VICTORIOUS

RIO 2016: TEAM GB'S HISTORIC OLYMPIC GAMES

This edition published in 2016

Copyright © Carlton Books Limited 2016

Carlton Books Limited
20 Mortimer Street
London W1T 3JW

A CIP catalogue record for this book is available from the British Library.

10 9 8 7 6 5 4 3 2 1

ISBN 978-1-78097-946-5

Project Manager: Chris Mitchell
Project Art Editor: Luke Griffin
Picture Research: Paul Langan
Production: Lisa Cook

Manufactured under license by Carlton Books Limited

Printed in Great Britain

Contents

The explosive Opening Ceremony for Rio 2016 began the Games in some style, and for Team GB it marked the start of a special Olympic Games.

Foreword

Welcome to *Victorious*. I hope you will enjoy reliving those inspirational moments which Team GB athletes provided for us all at the Rio 2016 Olympic Games.

Team GB's preparation for the Games, not only for the 17 days of the Games themselves but the build-up at our preparation camp in Belo Horizonte and, of course, the preceding four years was meticulous. It provided the perfect foundations for what was to follow.

Going into the Games it was always expressed that we hoped to better the medal total secured at Beijing 2008, with the BOA and UK Sport stating that eclipsing London 2012 was also a possibility. Of course, with sport, there are so many external factors which impact performance and the ultimate outcomes, so there can never be any guarantees.

However, as we reflect on a remarkable 67 medals, making history by being the first country to better their total at an away Games having previously hosted, my overarching feelings are ones of pride and satisfaction. Pride at the 366 athletes who represented their country with such great honour but also the satisfaction you feel when the incredible commitment and talent is rewarded after so many sacrifices and years of hard work.

For some, Rio 2016 will have been their last Olympic Games and I hope that representing Team GB will have fulfilled every expectation they had when they started out in their respective sports, with the ultimate goal of representing their nation at an Olympic Games.

However, what Rio also highlighted is that we have a tremendously talented group of athletes who will take their experiences forward to Tokyo 2020 where I am sure they will once again show the world what they are capable of.

It has been a great privilege to be the Chairman of the British Olympic Association and I wish all those athletes, current and aspiring, the very best of luck as they continue on their inspirational journeys to Tokyo 2020 and beyond, creating lifetime memories for us all.

Thank you for your support,

Lord Sebastian Coe

TEAM GB

BRING ON THE GREAT

After the incredible success of London 2012, it was difficult to imagine Team GB performing any better. Yet they found a way to improve, and Rio 2016 will go down in history as one of our greatest Olympic Games of all time.

The success of London 2012 had inspired a generation but trying to repeat it was a daunting task for the athletes selected to travel to Rio and proudly represent Great Britain and Northern Ireland on South American soil. The team of 366 athletes represented the third largest Team GB squad to travel to an overseas Games and the biggest since Barcelona in 1992.

UK Sport's National Lottery investment of £1.6million ensured the British Olympic Association could implement the ideal preparation camp in Belo Horizonte for Team GB athletes and support staff, providing world-class sporting facilities, accommodation and medical services coupled with similar climatic conditions to Rio, not to mention the advantage of being on the same time zone as Rio. The preparation camp was Team GB's largest pre-Games set-up to date and was used for final phase training, acclimatisation, hosting warm-up matches and rest and relaxation ahead of the short journey to Rio 2016.

Confidence was high as the Games began with a colourful Opening Ceremony but when Richard Kruse fell agonisingly short

Right: Flagbearer Andy Murray proudly leads Team GB at the Opening Ceremony.

Below: Games anticipation went up a notch at Team GB's official kit launch.

of winning a fencing medal on the first full day of action, few could have envisaged the British gold rush to come. Within hours, Adam Peaty had swept to the Olympic title in the Maria Lenk Aquatics Centre to begin a surge of success which would only stop when the total haul from London 2012 had been eclipsed.

While Peaty's success in the pool was only to be expected after a dominant season, other gold medals were less so and at times it was tough to keep track of the medal tally. Team GB's cycling team swept to glory in the velodrome, Sir Bradley Wiggins snaring a record eighth Olympic medal and Jason Kenny and Laura Trott, with five between them, anointed the nation's golden couple.

Britain celebrated a new diving hero in Jack Laugher, who took springboard gold alongside team-mate Chris Mears then went on to win an individual 3m silver. Incredible feats also occurred in the gymnastics hall, where Max Whitlock won bronze in the prestigious men's all-around, before winning Britain's first gold in the men's floor final and returned less than two hours later to make it a double on the men's pommel, where he nudged teammate Louis Smith into second place.

Andy Murray and Justin Rose rose admirably to the occassion of the intense Olympic stage with gold medals in tennis and golf respectively, while Giles Scott won sailing gold and Charlotte Dujardin triumphed again in the dressage. There were medals in the athletics arena for Jessica Ennis-Hill and Greg Rutherford and Mo Farah once again ruled supreme with another lung-bursting double to defend his 5,000m and 10,000m crowns.

At one end of the age spectrum was 58-year-old Nick Skelton, winning showjumping gold in his seventh Games, and at the other the youngest member of the entire Team GB delegation, Amy Tinkler, who took an unexpected bronze in the women's floor at the age of only 16.

Into its second week the British success story showed no signs of flagging as Alistair and Jonny Brownlee made the men's triathlon its predicted family affair by streaking to gold and silver. The taekwondo competition provided plenty of thrills and spills with Jade Jones clinching a historic second consecutive gold medal and the boxing delegation soaked up the punches with Nicola Adams once more reigning supreme. Josh Buatsi took a bronze and the programme almost ended on a high when super-heavyweight Joe Joyce was denied gold in a split-decision loss. It prevented the perfect ending but Joyce could still count himself every inch a part of the Team GB success story which ensured that post-London dip never materialized.

London 2012 – with 29 gold, 17 silver, 19 bronze and 65 medals in all – was Britain's most successful Games

"We've now enjoyed five successive Games of medal growth... It's an unbelievable achievement."

British Olympic Association chief executive **Bill Sweeney**.

Right: Adam Peaty tunes up at the Belo Horizonte preparation camp.

Below: Justin Rose was excited to be named during the golf team announcement at Royal Troon.

since 1908, which also took place in London. But that haul was surpassed on the final Saturday of the Games when Farah won the 5,000m and the women's 4x400m relay squad claimed bronze.

Team GB might have reached the total sooner, but there were 16 fourth-placed finishes to add to the success of those who had made it onto the podium. In the end, Team GB returned home with 67 medals – 27 gold, 23 silver and 17 bronze – across 18 sports and sat proudly behind the United States and above China in second place in the medal table. It was a fitting reward for years of dedication from the athletes and coaches involved, as well as two decades of hard work and investment in British and Northern Irish sport.

Bill Sweeney, chief executive of the British Olympic Association, said: "It has been a brilliant Games but this is not an overnight success. Thanks to the contribution of the National Lottery players via UK Sport and their investment, this is 20 years in the making and we've now enjoyed five successive Games of medal growth... it's an unbelievable achievement."

As with any Olympic Games, winning was not everything. Perhaps the most pertinent moment for a British athlete was the dignity displayed by taekwondo star Lutalo Muhammad after losing a gold medal with one second remaining on the clock. Muhammad's heartbreaking moment hardly hampered his achievement, nor the impact of taekwondo on a nation which went viral with the news. The fact he ended with Olympic silver, rather than gold, hung around his neck is neither here nor there to the children who saw the sport and nurture a new-found desire to high-kick for a living.

Others will have been inspired by long-awaited British success in other sports. Chris Langridge and Marcus Ellis teamed up to win Team GB's first Olympic badminton medal since 2004, while the women's hockey team won gold for the first time.

The Games in Rio produced many new stars and helped enhance the reputations of others. Simone Biles, Usain Bolt, Kaori Icho, Katie Ledecky, Michael Phelps would figure in most discussions about the key players in Rio, but those discussions could last a while. Abbey D'Agostino and Nikki Hamblin helping each other to finish the 5,000 metres after falls, Wayde van Niekerk upstaging Bolt on 100m final night by obliterating Michael Johnson's 400m record, Neymar winning football-mad Brazil's most cherished gold in a shoot-out, Fiji's first Olympic medal in the first ever rugby sevens event. It is quite a list.

At the Closing Ceremony, International Olympic Committee president Thomas Bach was also quick to herald the example of the first ever team of refugees at the Games, saying they were a "symbol of hope to millions of refugees". But his key message was that Rio had pulled it off. "These were marvellous Games in the marvellous city, and they leave a unique legacy," he said. "History will talk about a Rio before the Olympic Games and a much better Rio after the Olympic Games."

Team GB's large representation caught the eye in shoes with flashing lights, which many took off and waved during one of the dance numbers. It was a fitting end to a Games at which so many Team GB athletes shone on the greatest stage.

"History will talk about a Rio before the Olympic Games and a much better Rio after the Olympics."

International Olympic Committee president **Thomas Bach**.

Aquatics

The indoor swimming events took place at the Olympic Aquatics Centre, a temporary venue on the Olympic Park in Barra da Tijuca, with Fort Copacabana hosting the open water competitions. Diving and synchronised swimming were staged at the Maria Lenk Aquatics Centre.

Events

SWIMMING
Men's & Women's 50m freestyle
Men's & Women's 100m freestyle
Men's & Women's 400m freestyle
Women's 800m freestyle
Men's 1500m freestyle
Men's & Women's 100m backstroke
Men's & Women's 200m backstroke
Men's & Women's 100m breaststroke
Men's & Women's 200m breaststroke
Men's & Women's 100m butterfly
Men's & Women's 200m butterfly
Men's & Women's 200m individual medley
Men's & Women's 400m individual medley
Men's & Women's 4x100m freestyle relay
Men's & Women's 4x200m freestyle relay
Men's & Women's 4x100m medley relay
Men's & Women's 10km marathon

DIVING
Men's & Women's 3m springboard
Men's & Women's 10m platform
Men's & Women's synchronised 3m springboard
Men's & Women's synchronised 10m platform

SYNCHRONISED SWIMMING
Women's duet
Women's team

World and Olympic champion Adam Peaty on his way to gold and a new world record.

Diving

Jack Laugher and Chris Mears led a terrific Team GB performance in the pool as they secured Britain's first Olympic diving gold, to add to a further silver and bronze medal.

Team GB claimed a record haul of three Olympic medals in the diving pool as Jack Laugher emerged as the new darling of the sport. Tom Daley has been at the forefront of bringing diving into the consciousness of the country since he made a baby-faced Olympic debut in Beijing at the age of 14, but Laugher has picked up the baton.

The 21-year-old Yorkshireman had previously been touted by four-time Olympic champion Greg Louganis as one of the most promising divers in the world and he delivered on that promise in full on a teary evening alongside his teammate, and close friend, Chris Mears. The duo combined to break China's dominance in the diving pool – the Asian nation won every other gold on offer – but more significantly won Team GB's first Olympic diving title

with a breathless performance in the men's 3m synchronised springboard.

If the success was unexpected it served only to underline the size of their achievement when the emotion of the moment brought Laugher to tears in front of the TV cameras. Only four years earlier, with Louganis' high-profile endorsement ringing in his ears, Laugher had been left completely distraught as he crashed out in the first round of the 3m springboard.

The then-teenager was too upset to speak to the media in the aftermath, but in the four years that followed he used the setback as motivation for his return to the Olympic stage. The results were not just a spectacular gold but also a silver in the same individual event that had ended so cruelly for him in London as he became Team GB's most decorated Olympic diver in the space of a couple of days.

He admitted refocusing after the high of the synchro gold had been difficult, saying: "It was really hard to reset because that is the pinnacle of my entire career so far. Olympic gold is just something to be cherished for a lifetime so it was really hard coming

off that mountain top and dropping back down to getting up at 6am and doing training. But I really focused well."

Mears's own story was just as compelling with the part-time DJ – who has worked with Nicole Scherzinger – lucky just to be alive after he almost died following a junior event in Australia seven years ago. Mears was given only a five per cent chance of survival, and was in a coma for three days, and after his family made the panicked journey halfway around the world to be at his bedside they have since seen him embark on a remarkable journey to the very top of his sport.

Daley had already kickstarted Team GB's record haul in Rio when he teamed up with Daniel Goodfellow in the platform synchro to secure a bronze medal to sit alongside the one he won in London in the individual.

While he was unable to go better than his London bronze in the individual platform – despite topping the charts after the first round – Daley was still able to leave Rio knowing his legacy for British diving has been reinforced further following the team's record Olympic Games.

> ## "I know everyone's so proud of me back home but I'm just a normal kid from Yorkshire. This is my job and I love it every single day."
>
> **Jack Laugher.**

Above left: Jack Laugher (left) and Chris Mears show off Team GB's first ever diving gold medals after winning the men's synchronised 3m springboard.

Opposite page: Officials were puzzled when the water in the Maria Lenk Aquatic Centre diving pool turned green.

Above: Laugher collected a second medal when he took silver in the individual 3m springboard event.

Left: Tom Daley and Daniel Goodfellow finished third in the platform synchro diving, Daley's second Olympic bronze medal at successive Games.

Green and gold

The pool may have turned green but it did not stop Jack Laugher and Chris Mears winning a first Olympic diving gold for Britain in the men's three metres springboard. Helped by the typically British weather conditions, the pair scored 454.32 to leave China needing better than 93.84 to win with the penultimate dive of the competition. The Chinese pair faltered, though, scoring 83.22 to spark jubilant celebrations among the British contingent.

Teen triumph

Ren Qian was the youngest Olympic champion in Rio after winning the women's 10 metres platform final at the age of 15. The Chinese prodigy produced five stunning dives to beat her 17-year-old team-mate Si Yajie as China were once again dominant in the diving pool. Ren never received a mark lower than 8.5 and her final two dives produced three perfect 10s as she kept her cool on her Olympic debut.

Swimming

Team GB's swimmers stepped up to the plate impressively with a series of strong performances in Rio, led by Adam Peaty's brilliant gold medal and repeated world record swims.

It took Team GB until the end of day two to win their first medal at the Olympic Games but as soon as Adam Peaty dived into the water there was never any doubt that the duck would be broken in golden fashion. The 21-year-old from Uttoxeter headed to Rio as the world, European and Commonwealth champion in the 100m breaststroke.

There was huge expectation on his young shoulders but confidence rather than nerves imbued Peaty as he broke his own world record in the heats. Given that no other man in history had ever dipped beneath 58 seconds, his time of 57.55 made him appear unbeatable, and so it proved. He swam only a fraction slower in the semi-finals and then blasted his way to a time of 57.13 in the final, winning what is a sprint event by an incredible margin of more than 1.5 seconds.

Medals in the pool have been historically hard to come by for Team GB and Peaty's gold was the first for a male swimmer since

Adrian Moorhouse won the same event in Seoul 1988. Four years ago in London swimming ended the Games with only three medals – two for Rebecca Adlington and one for Michael Jamieson – and none of them gold. In Rio, Team GB finished fifth in the swimming medal table with one gold and five silvers. Two of those belonged to Welsh swimmer Jazz Carlin, who missed out on London through illness but made up for it in brilliant fashion. The 26-year-old finished best of the rest behind extraordinary American Katie Ledecky in the 400m and 800m freestyle, with her first medal coming hot on the heels of Peaty's gold.

By the fourth night, Britain had already eclipsed their London efforts after Siobhan-Marie O'Connor, in the 200m individual medley, and the men's 4x200m freestyle relay team both claimed silver medals. O'Connor, who made her Olympic debut in London aged 16, set a new British record, with her achievement all the more impressive considering she suffers from the debilitating colon condition ulcerative colitis.

Team GB's final medal came in the men's 4x100m medley relay as Peaty once again stole the show. Taking over from Chris Walker-Hebborn in sixth place following the backstroke leg, Peaty surged into the lead with an incredible split of 56.59.

"I just love to push myself every single day. Hopefully that will, in another Olympic final, push me to a new barrier."

Adam Peaty has already set himself new goals.

Above: Jazz Carlin had to contend with the shadow of remarkable American Katie Ledecky in the 400m and 800m freestyle taking silver in both events.

Left: Carlin, Ledecky and bronze medal winner Leah Smith on the 400m podium.

Opposite page: Team GB's swimming star Adam Peaty shows off his 100m breaststroke gold medal.

Below: Siobhan-Marie O'Connor heads for silver in the 200m individual medley.

A Michael Phelps-inspired USA proved too strong in the end but Peaty showed that his target of going beneath 57 seconds for the individual event was well within his grasp. The City of Derby swimmer is also the world champion and record holder over 50m, which is not an Olympic event, and has set his sights on challenging over 200m in Tokyo in four years' time.

A great week for Team GB could have been even better taking into account the seven fourth-placed finishes. They varied from the surprised and delighted, like Max Litchfield in the 400m individual medley, to agonising near misses for Hannah Miley, Andrew Willis, Fran Halsall and Chloe Tutton. There was further disappointment in the open-water events, where Beijing silver medallist Keri-anne Payne finished seventh and Jack Burnell was furious to be disqualified after being in medal contention.

The USA dominated in the pool, led by Phelps and Ledecky. Having initially retired following London 2012, Phelps returned to the sport in 2014, spurred on principally by one aim: winning back the 200m butterfly title so memorably taken from him by South African Chad Le Clos in 2012.

He did that and also won golds in the 200m individual medley and three relays as well as silver in the 100m butterfly, where he, Le Clos and Laszlo Cseh ended up in a three-way tie for silver behind Singapore's Joseph Schooling. Phelps, who was supported poolside by baby son Boomer, ended his Olympic career – and he insisted this really was it – with 28 medals, 23 of them gold.

The 31-year-old's record-breaking feats included ending Leonidas of Rhodes' 2168-year reign as the only man to win 12 individual titles. Phelps teamed up with fellow veteran Ryan Lochte to win the 4x200m freestyle relay.

If Phelps and Lochte are now the past, 19-year-old Ledecky is both the present and the future. Having stunned Adlington to win gold in the 800m in London, Ledecky added four further Olympic titles to her collection along with a silver in the 4x100m freestyle relay.

Above: Team GB's 4x200m freestyle relay silver medallists, from left, James Guy, Duncan Scott, Dan Wallace and Stephen Milne.

Left: Jack Burnell (centre, red cap) was angered by his disqualification from the 10km open water swim.

Right: Michael Phelps celebrates gold in the 200m butterfly, the medal which inspired his comeback.

Below: Adam Peaty, Duncan Scott, Chris Walker-Hebborn and James Guy with their silver medals after the 4x100m medley relay final.

Below right: Katie Ledecky with her 800m freestyle gold medal.

For the record

World Records

Swimming – Men's 100m breaststroke
Adam Peaty (Team GB) 57.13

Swimming – Men's 100m backstroke
Ryan Murphy (USA) 51.85 (in 4x100m medley relay)

Swimming – Women's 400m individual medley
Katinka Hosszu (Hungary) 4:26.36

Swimming – Women's 4x100m freestyle relay
Australia 3:30.65

Swimming – Women's 100m butterfly
Sarah Sjostrom (Sweden) 55.48

Swimming – Women's 400m freestyle
Katie Ledecky (USA) 3:56.46

Swimming – Women's 800m freestyle
Katie Ledecky (USA) 8:04.79

Olympic Records

Swimming – Men's 200m breaststroke
Ippei Watanabe (Japan) 2:07.22

Swimming – Men's 100m butterfly
Joseph Schooling (Singapore) 50.39

Swimming – Men's 4x100m medley relay
USA 3:27.95

Swimming – Women's 200m individual medley
Katinka Hosszu (Hungary) 2:06.58

Swimming – Women's 100m breaststroke
Lilly King (USA) 1:04.93

Swimming – Women's 100m freestyle
Simone Manuel (USA) & Penny Oleksiak (Canada) 52.70 (dead heat)

Record breaker Peaty

Adam Peaty was in a class of his own in the 100m breaststroke final, leading the field from the start and pulling away to smash his own world record by more than 1.5 seconds to claim gold. He was already world, European and Commonwealth champion and, at only 21, there could yet be much more to come from one of British sport's golden boys.

Phelps regains title

The USA won 16 golds in the pool, only one fewer than the rest of the world combined. The most coveted was the men's 200m butterfly, a title won by Michael Phelps in Athens and Beijing but taken from him by Chad Le Clos in London. Securing its return motivated Phelps' comeback and there was no doubt what it meant to him to touch first. Le Clos missed out on a medal.

Synchronised Swimming

Olivia Federici and Katie Clark secured a 17th place finish for Team GB in the synchronised swimming, which was a fine achievement for two athletes who had only been out of retirement for a year.

Having come out of retirement for another crack at the Olympic Games, Olivia Federici and Katie Clark finished 17th in Rio. The duo had initially quit the sport in 2013, but made a return two years later and secured a quota place in the duet event. For 26-year-old Federici it was a third Olympic appearance, while both athletes were also part of the squad which finished sixth in the team event at London 2012. Clark said: "When I had the meeting to say I was retiring, my coach told me I had more potential and more left in me and that stuck with me. At the time it felt right to leave, but when I thought about the opportunity to come back, I'd never been part of a duet before and I really wanted to push myself that little bit further."

Federici added: "I wanted to get back to the sport that I love. I had a break and experienced life, but I had a really positive feeling about coming back and Rio was always going to be a big challenge. Being an athlete is always a very big sacrifice, not just for me but for my family, and I didn't want to come back and embarrass myself by not being good enough. But it has all definitely been worth it."

Clark and Federici were keen to provide Team GB with an Olympic presence in order to inspire the next generation. A score of 79.9667 for their duet free routine left the pair 18th, but they climbed a spot with an improved 80.7650 in the technical, an effort which pleased Federici.

"We really wanted to go out there and really smash it," she said. "Our coaches are happy and it felt like a really good swim which is pleasing. We gave it our all, it was very good. People often still think about the very old style of synchronised swimming with the athletes floating around in pretty patterns, but now it's very fast, powerful and dynamic."

Russian pair Natalia Ishchenko and Svetlana Romashina dominated from the start and took gold with a score of 194.9910, 2.6222 ahead of Chinese runners-up Xuechen Huang and Wenyan Sun and 6.9363 clear of Japan's bronze medallists Yukiko Inui and Risako Mitsui. The team event saw a repeat result, with Russia being awarded a couple of perfect 10s as they won gold with a score of 196.1439, with China once more distant runners-up and Japan third.

"We've had a much bigger intake into synchronised swimming which is really positive and we've got a lot of talented swimmers coming up which is exciting for the sport."

Olivia Federici.

Above: The Russian team on their way to team gold to complete a synchronised swimming double.

Left: Japan's bronze-medal winning team.

Opposite page: Team GB's Katie Clark (left) and Olivia Federici came out of retirement to compete in Rio.

Russians rampant

Russia's dominance continued as they won a fifth consecutive team title, scoring two perfect 10s in the process. They were more than three points clear of China, who won silver for the second Olympic Games running, with Japan pipping Ukraine to bronze. Natalia Ishchenko and Svetlana Romashina successfully defended the pair title they won at London 2012 as the pair event also saw Russia finish ahead of China and Japan.

Archery

Hosting the archery was the Sambodromo, traditionally used for samba school parades during Carnival and designed by famous Brazilian architect Oscar Niemeyer.

Events

Men's & Women's individual
Men's & Women's team

Patrick Huston was the first Team GB athlete in action at Rio 2016 as the archery ranking rounds began before the Opening Ceremony.

Archery

Archers Patrick Huston and Naomi Folkard were the first members of Team GB in action at Rio 2016 and there was a best-ever individual finish for Folkard at her fourth Olympic Games.

At the start of the Rio 2016 archery campaign, Olympic debutant Patrick Huston was relishing having the duty of kicking things off for the whole of Team GB at the Games. By the end, the experienced Naomi Folkard could reflect on marking the probable conclusion of her Olympic career with her finest run at that level.

Before the Opening Ceremony at the Maracana Stadium started later that day, August 5 saw Huston and Folkard take part in the men's and women's individual rankings rounds. Northern Irishman Huston was thrilled to be the first Briton to compete at the Games, something he regarded as fitting for his particular discipline.

"Historically, archers in battle were always the first to attack, so it fits in quite nicely and it is really great to be the first person doing

that," the 20-year-old said. Huston went on to rank 38th of 64 as first-placed Kim Woo-jin of South Korea registered a world-record score of 700 from 72 arrows.

The following week Huston beat 27th-ranked Dutchman Rick van der Ven 6-4 in the first round, before losing in the last 32 to South Korea's Ku Bon-chan, who had been sixth and would go on to claim the gold medal. Huston said: "It's made me thirstier for subsequent Games. I think Rio 2016 is a big stepping-stone to Tokyo."

Leamington Spa's Folkard, who would turn 33 in September, came 23rd in the ranking round. She then got past Ika Yuliana Rochmawati of Indonesia, Kaori Kawanaka of Japan and Brazil's Ane Marcelle dos Santos before she was defeated in the quarter-finals by South Korea's

second-ranked Chang Hye-jin – again, a Briton coming unstuck at the hands of the archer who would later be crowned champion.

It made for a commendable potential Olympic sign-off for Folkard, who reached the last 16 at Athens 2004 and Beijing 2008, the last 32 at London 2012, and had already signalled this would be her final Games. Folkard said after her loss to Chang: "To finish top eight in the Olympic Games is something I couldn't have dreamt of a few months ago. I'm not planning on continuing. I've been a full-time archer for 11 years and I need a life. I want to get into coaching. I will always be involved in the sport. You never know, they might persuade me to come back but I need at least one year out."

"It is absolutely inspiring to be the first Briton leading the charge."

Patrick Huston on getting Team GB's Rio 2016 campaign under way.

Left: Patrick Huston was delighted that archers opened Team GB's Olympic Games.

Above: South Korean fans revel in their country's domination of the archery competition.

Below left: Naomi Folkard had her best finish in her fourth and probably final Olympic Games.

Below: Chang Hye-jin takes a leaf from Mo Farah's book as she celebrates her gold medal.

The right notes

Patrick Huston was helped through his first Games experience by a series of motivational notes inspired by the former Olympic shooter and now sports psychologist Lanny Bassham. Focused by notes including "I am the 2016 Olympic champion", Huston said: "I have notes pasted up on my wall in the Olympic Village and it is just something to inspire me and keep me focused. The mental aspect is crucial in archery."

Korea path

Kim Woo-jin got the Games off to a flying start with a world-record 700 score from 72 arrows. The South Korean's historic total beat by a single point the record set by his compatriot Im Dong-hyun at the equivalent stage of the London 2012 Games. Kim said: "I practised more than everyone else and I gave my best in the entire round."

Athletics

All the athletics events apart from the race walks and marathons were held at the Olympic Stadium in the Engenho de Dentro district of Rio de Janeiro.

Events

FIELD
Men's & Women's long jump
Men's & Women's triple jump
Men's & Women's high jump
Men's & Women's pole vault
Men's & Women's shot put
Men's & Women's discus throw
Men's & Women's javelin throw
Men's & Women's hammer throw

COMBINED
Men's decathlon
Women's heptathlon

ROAD
Men's & Women's marathon
Men's & Women's 20km walk
Men's 50km walk

TRACK
Men's & Women's 100m
Men's & Women's 200m
Men's & Women's 400m
Men's & Women's 800m
Men's & Women's 1,500m
Men's & Women's 5,000m
Men's & Women's 10,000m
Men's 110m hurdles
Women's 100m hurdles
Men's & Women's 400m hurdles
Men's & Women's 3,000m steeplechase
Men's & Women's 4 x 100m relay
Men's & Women's 4 x 400m relay

Mo Farah won the men's 5,000m and 10,000m for the second successive Games to complete a remarkable 'double double'.

Athletics

Rio 2016 saw Mo Farah's golden 'double double', confirming him as one of the greatest runners of all-time, alongside a series of fantastic results from Team GB athletes which led to an impressive seven-medal tally.

"So many athletes just don't know when it's the time to retire and I don't want to be that athlete who fizzles out. I want to end on a high."

Jessica Ennis-Hill.

Track & Field

Team GB's athletics big three came to Rio looking to defend their titles and Mo Farah's long-distance domination continued in some style. The inspiring athlete, who had already achieved enough to be viewed as one of the greatest athletes to ever perform for Team GB, blazed a trail to sporting immortality. Farah's breathtaking defence of his 5,000 and 10,000m titles saw him become the first British track and field athlete to win four Olympic gold medals, and he maintained his unprecedented spell of long-distance domination by landing his ninth straight global crown, stretching back to the 2011 World Championships in Daegu.

The 33-year-old Londoner, set to move over to the road after the 2017 World Championships in London, is the second man to retain both 5,000m and 10,000m Olympic crowns after Flying Finn Lasse Viren in 1976, while his total haul of four golds is twice that of any other British track and field athlete.

Meanwhile, Jess Ennis-Hill and Greg Rutherford came to the Games looking to defend the gold medals they had won four years previously at London 2012. For Ennis-Hill in particular this was always going to be a difficult task, albeit one she was extremely excited to take on. The 30-year-old had carried the weight of a nation on her shoulders four years ago as the poster girl for the home Olympic Games and delivered in style. Her path since then, though, had been far from straightforward, with Achilles problems and the small matter of the birth of her son Reggie in the summer of 2014.

Above: Team GB hero Mo Farah jumps for joy after winning the 5,000m.

Opposite page: Jessica Ennis-Hill's score was her best since winning gold at London 2012.

Above: Sophie Hitchon shows her delight at gaining bronze in the hammer.

Below: Team GB bronze medallist Greg Rutherford in action in the long jump.

She headed to Brazil as the reigning world champion but history was against her. No British woman had retained an Olympic track and field title while only two other woman had ever won Olympic gold, had a baby and then returned to successfully defend their title. The Sheffield athlete faced the tallest of tall orders. In the end, she did all anyone could ask of her, achieving her best overall score since landing gold at London 2012, of 6,775 points. Her performance alone was a cause for celebration and an incredible achievement. Ultimately, it was not quite enough to land the gold medal, but still resulted in a highly commendable silver.

Belgian Nafissatou Thiam, nine years younger than the Briton, produced five personal bests from seven events to win by 35 points. Ennis-Hill went into the final discipline, the 800m, needing to run 9.47 seconds quicker than Thiam to make up a deficit of 142 points. She produced a hugely gutsy display of front-running to give herself the best possible chance and came home in 2:09.07 but Thiam's time of 2:16.54 was enough. Ennis-Hill's tears at the end were born of the fact she knew this was likely to be her final competition, with retirement now on the cards. Her team-mate Katarina Johnson-Thompson also wept, but her tears were of frustration after finishing sixth on 6,523 points.

In the long jump, Rutherford was looking to land his fifth straight major title, having picked up Commonwealth, world and two European golds in an unbeaten run at majors dating back to 2013. However, a dramatic competition saw him finish in third as American Jeff Henderson took gold with a final-round effort of 8.38m, denying South Africa's Luvo Manyonga by a centimetre. In fact, Rutherford was down in fourth until sealing his podium place by leaping out to 8.29m on his final jump. Not that the Milton Keynes man was happy, saying: "I don't come here to win bronze medals, silver medals or whatever else. I come here to win."

Rutherford felt circumstances had conspired against him with his fourth-round jump initially ruled to be a foul but then reinstated. The distance of 8.26m would not have changed the result but would have put him into the lead at the time and allowed him to put pressure on the rest of the field.

Britain's biggest surprise medal at the Olympic Stadium came courtesy of former ballet dancer Sophie Hitchon, who broke her own national record with the very last throw of the hammer competition. Hitchon launched the hammer out to 74.54m to move from sixth place to third and become the first Briton to win an Olympic medal in the discipline since 1924. "A bit special" was how she described it after an emotional and joyous celebration which Team GB fans could not help but take pride in.

Back on the track, there were bronze medals for both the women's 4x100m and 4x400m relay teams, which completed Team GB's track and field medal haul in Rio. Christine Ohuruogu anchored the 4x400m quartet to become only the second British track and field athlete, after Steve Backley, to win a medal at three consecutive Olympic Games.

Ohuruogu, who won individual gold at Beijing 2008 and silver at London 2012, also hinted at retirement after finishing fifth in her individual 400m semi-final in Rio. There will clearly be a changing of the guard.

There is plenty of optimism about the up-and-coming generation and it is not misplaced. Heptathlete Johnson-Thompson, middle-distance runners Laura Muir and Lynsey Sharp, sprinters Dina Asher-Smith and Adam Gemili, plus one-lap specialist Matt Hudson-Smith, to name just a few,

Opposite page: 4x100m bronze medallists Daryll Neita, Asher-Smith, Desiree Henry and Asha Philip ran an impressive new national record.

Above: 4x400m medallists Christine Ohuruogu, Emily Diamond, Anyika Onuora and Eilidh Doyle celebrate their medal-winning performance.

Below: Adam Gemili (left) finished fourth in an incredibly tight 200m finsh, only three-thousandths of a second from claiming a medal.

Right Lynsey Sharp produced a career-best time in the women's 800m final, finishing sixth in a race won by favourite Castor Semenya.

have bags of potential and time on their side. There are big names, and personalities, to replace, but this generation appear to be up to the task, and will already be looking ahead to Tokyo 2020 as the arena to showcase their talents to the world.

Farah won his first event in Rio, the 10,000m, the hard way after falling to the track following a trip by training partner Galen Rupp. He recovered to respond to the challenge laid down by Paul Tanui, his trademark burst down the home straight taking him past the Kenyan and over the line in 27 minutes 5.17 seconds. The manner of his victory, which could so easily have slipped away, left Farah hugely emotional. He had eclipsed the Olympic greats of double champions Sebastian Coe, Daley Thompson and Kelly Holmes and more was to come.

One week later, Farah avoided

any such drama in the 5,000m final, pulling clear down the home straight to cross the line in 13:03.30 after producing a whirlwind final lap of 52.83 seconds to hold off the challenge of American Paul Kipkemoi Chelimo and Ethiopian Hagos Gebrhiwet. Chelimo was subsequently disqualified, meaning Gebrhiwet took the silver and another American, 41-year-old Bernard Lagat, the bronze, while Farah's GB teammate Andrew Butchart ran the race of his life in his first major championships. The 24-year-old took nearly five seconds off the Scottish record of 13.13:30 he set in late May to finish sixth in 13.08.61.

Fittingly, Farah's medal was the one that brought Team GB level with their medal haul from London 2012 of 65, a total they surpassed a few minutes later when the women's

4x400m relay team claimed bronze.

Team GB's women won their first Olympic 4x100m medal in 32 years as Asha Philip, Desiree Henry, Asher-Smith and Daryll Neita set a new national record en route to bronze. They arrived in Rio as strong medal hopes having become the country's first team to go sub-42 seconds at the Anniversary Games the previous month and that 41.81 run was beaten as they took a first medal since Los Angeles 1984 in 41.77.

Soon after Farah had retained 5,000m gold to secure his dream 'double double', the 4x400m relay girls took to the track and Eilidh Doyle, Anyika Onuora, Emily Diamond and Ohuruogu, the last British athletes in action at the Olympic Stadium, brought the curtain down in style, winning a first women's medal in the event since Barcelona 1992 by crossing the line third in 3:25.88.

Earlier the same evening, 26-year-old Sharp produced a lifetime best run of 1:57.69 to finish sixth in the women's 800m final, won by South Africa's red-hot favourite Caster Semenya. Muir, 23, went into the women's 1,500m final as a real medal hope after breaking Holmes's 12-year-old British record at the London Anniversary Games the previous month and, although the Scot was in third place and on the tail of the leaders with 200m to go, she faded to finish seventh behind gold-medal winner Faith Kipyegon of Kenya.

Sprint duo Gemili, 22, and Asher-Smith, 20, offer serious hope for the future. Former footballer Gemili finished an agonising fourth in the men's 200m final, three-thousandths of a second behind France's bronze medal winner Christophe Lemaitre in a time of 20.12, while Asher-Smith ran her fastest time of the year in her first Olympic final, the women's 200m, in 22.31 – only 0.24 seconds outside her personal best.

Hudson-Smith, 21, produced a blistering finish in the semi-final of the men's 400m to finish second in a new

"In that split second I thought four years had gone. And it wasn't in my control. Mentally I was dazed when I crossed the line. I don't get emotional, but I did."

Mo Farah reflects on his dramatic 10,000m triumph.

personal best of 44.48 before coming last in a historic final that was won by South African sensation Wayde van Niekerk. He produced the stand-out track performance of the Games to smash Michael Johnson's 17-year-old world record of 43.18 in a stunning time of 43.03, even managing the rare feat of upstaging Usain Bolt's third 100m gold a few minutes later.

Bolt's magnificent 'triple triple' in the 100m, 200m and 4x100m relay is unlikely to be repeated but new world stars will emerge on the track in time for Tokyo 2020 and Team GB will strive to maintain their place in the thick of the action.

Road

Race walking is Tom Bosworth's chosen discipline, and the talented athlete has made the sport his home, adding race-winning dances and victory celebrations to his ever-improving performances.

The 26-year-old went into the 20km walk in Rio as a 100/1 outsider but looked capable of pulling off one of the great Olympic shocks until fading over the final laps of the beachside course. The Kent athlete led the field for much of the first half of the race and was in medal contention until only a few kilometres from the finish before crossing the line in sixth place.

His time of 1:20:13 still smashed his own British record, set back in March, by a whopping 28 seconds, offering plenty of reason for optimism for the Tokyo Olympic Games in four years' time. China celebrated a one-two, with Zhen Wang taking gold ahead of team-mate Zelin Cai.

Bosworth said: "I felt good and was comfortable with the pace I was going but I knew I had the best in the world behind me and I knew they would catch me but I just tried to hold on. I dropped down to ninth at one point but I thought 'I've not led the race for this long to finish outside the top eight' and just went for it."

There was better to come for Bosworth as four days later he got engaged. He posted a picture on Twitter of him down on one knee proposing to his partner Harry Dineley

Top: Team GB's Tom Bosworth led the 20km walk for the first half of the race.

Above: Team GB's marathon-running brothers Callum and Derek Hawkins.

on Copacabana Beach. Above it were the words: "He said YES!!!"

There was another breakthrough British performance in the men's marathon as Callum Hawkins, racing alongside older brother Derek, came an impressive ninth out of 140 finishers. The 24-year-old led the race at the midway point before coming home in 2:11:52 as Kenya's Eliud Kipchoge took a dominant gold in 2:08:44. Derek did not fare as well as he came

home in 114th place.

In the women's marathon, Team GB's Alyson Dixon and Sonia Samuels were 28th and 30th respectively as London Marathon champion Jemima Sumgong won Kenya's first gold in the event. The gold medal in the women's walk went to Liu Hong of China, with the world champion edging out Mexico's Maria Guadalupe Gonzalez by just two seconds.

Above: The Triple Triple. Bolt's final Games were as brilliantly emphatic as the previous two, confirming his place as the greatest sprinter ever.

Below: Mo Farah recovered from a dangerous stumble to win golds in both the 5,000 and 10,000m.

Top right: In an exciting finish, the popular London 2012 champion Jess Ennis-Hill was just pipped to gold in the heptathlon.

Opposite top: Wayde van Niekerk became an instant superstar when he crossed the line in a record time in the 400m.

Opposite bottom: Sophie Hitchon became the first British woman to win a medal in the hammer throw.

For the record

World Records

Athletics – Women's 10,000m
Almaz Ayana (Ethiopia) 29:17.45

Athletics – Men's 400m
Wayde Van Niekerk (South Africa) 43.03

Athletics – Women's hammer throw
Anita Wlodarczyk (Poland) 82.29m

Olympic Records

Athletics – Men's pole vault
Thiago da Silva (Brazil) 6.03m

Athletics – Men's 3,000m steeplechase
Conseslus Kipruto (Kenya) 8:03.28

Athletics – Men's decathlon
Ashton Eaton (USA) 8,893 points

Athletics – Women's 5,000m
Vivian Jepkemoi Cheruiyot (Kenya) 14:26.17

Athletics – Men's shot put
Ryan Crouser (USA) 22.52m

Mighty Mo

Mo Farah was determined nobody would deny him a fourth Olympic gold medal as he completed the long-distance double at a second straight Games by storming to 5,000m glory. A week after being tripped on the way to 10,000m gold, Farah avoided more drama and burst clear down the home straight to cross the line in 13:03.30.

Farah stated ahead of the race that he needed a fourth gold for his son Hussein, with his three others dedicated to his older three children. He said: "Now all my four kids have got one medal each and when I'm one day gone they will have something."

Lap of honour

Wayde van Niekerk is the new one-lap king and star of the track after smashing Michael Johnson's 17-year-old 400m world record en route to a remarkable Olympic gold medal.

The 24-year-old South African even managed to upstage the legendary Usain Bolt, who won the 100m final later on the same night. While the Jamaican's triumph got the Brazilian crowd on their feet, it was Van Niekerk who left them open-mouthed. His astonishing time of 43.03 seconds obliterated Johnson's mark of 43.18 from 1999 and was made all the more remarkable by the fact his run came from lane eight.

Badminton

Badminton has been played at the Olympic Games since Barcelona 1992, with mixed doubles added to the programme four years later in Atlanta. Five titles were up for grabs at Riocentro Pavilion 4.

Events

Men's & Women's singles
Men's & Women's doubles
Mixed doubles

Marcus Ellis and Chris Langridge (right) in action against China's Chai Biao and Hong Wei during the men's doubles bronze medal match.

Badminton

Team GB were represented in all five disciplines for the first time since 2004 and a gruelling year of qualifying for Chris Langridge and Marcus Ellis paid off when they defied their world ranking to claim a bronze medal.

Chris Langridge and Marcus Ellis beat the odds as they secured Team GB's first badminton medal at an Olympic Games for 12 years. The pair arrived in Rio ranked 22 in the world and left with a bronze medal after beating China's Chai Biao and Hong Wei 21-18 19-21 21-10 in the men's doubles at Riocentro. It was a performance to prove their quality as they stepped onto an Olympic podium just two years after their partnership was forged.

"On our day, we know we are so capable, and I am so glad we could show it," three-time Commonwealth Games medallist Langridge said. "We got to the quarter-finals of the worlds, and this will give us the belief that we shouldn't be 22 in the world, we should be top ten. From the age of ten, I have been dreaming of an Olympic medal, and now we have done it. It is insane."

The pair had to do it the hard way to fulfil that childhood dream as their hopes were almost dashed on only the second day of competition. After losing a difficult group-stage opener against London 2012 silver medallists Mathias Boe and Carsten Mogensen, they had to fight from a set down against third seeds Kim Gi-jung and Kim Sa-rang. A pulsating second set was won 25-23, which proved the catalyst for their run to the bronze

medal as they sneaked out of their group, before a straight-sets win over Japan's Hiroyuki Endo and Kenichi Hayakawa in the quarter-finals. While eventual gold medallists Fu Haifeng and Zhang Nan beat them in the semi-finals, Langridge and Ellis were not to be denied in the bronze-medal match as they streaked away in the deciding set.

"We could have easily folded following the second set after being so close to taking it," Ellis said. "I am very proud of how we came out in the third." It was Team GB's first badminton medal since Gail Emms and Nathan Robertson took silver in the mixed doubles at Athens.

Husband and wife pair Chris and Gabrielle Adcock had hoped to replicate that performance and add to their Commonwealth title in the mixed doubles despite being handed a 'group of death'. They were pooled with the silver and bronze medallists from London 2012 and, while they overcame fourth-seeded Danish pair Joachim Fischer Nielsen and Christinna Pedersen, the quality of the group meant they did not progress.

Team GB's thirteenth seed Rajiv Ouseph won both his group-stage games in the men's singles event, before falling to Danish bronze medallist Viktor Axelsen in the quarter-finals.

"We are not just proud of ourselves. We are proud we've managed to do it for our sport. All the guys back home can take something from what we have done."

Marcus Ellis.

Above: Husband and wife team Gabrielle and Chris Adcock on their way to victory over fourth seeds Joachim Fischer Nielsen and Christinna Pedersen.

Right: China's Zhang Nan (left) and Fu Haifeng celebrate men's doubles gold.

Opposite page: Marcus Ellis and Chris Langridge (right) with their bronze medals from the men's doubles.

Below: Rajiv Ouseph in action against eventual bronze medallist Viktor Axelsen.

Right to review

Chris Langridge and Marcus Ellis faced an anxious wait to learn whether they had won an Olympic medal. Langridge called for a review on the crucial point, confident his serve had landed in, and was proved to be correct. "I can't even describe how I felt after we saw that," said Ellis, who dropped to the floor in tears, while there were jubilant scenes among the support team and in the stands.

Sweet Carolina

No woman from outside Asia had ever won an Olympic singles title, but that changed when Spain's Carolina Marin beat PV Sindhu of India in the women's tournament. Her 19-21 21-12 21-15 victory secured a gold medal to add to her world and European titles and she said: "I'm very excited. It is amazing my dream has come true. I just had to believe in myself."

Boxing

The newly-built Riocentro Pavilion 6 was the home to all the boxing in Rio and there were 13 competitions taking place, including three for women after female fighters made their Games debut at London 2012.

Events

Men's light-flyweight
Men's flyweight
Men's bantamweight
Men's lightweight
Men's light-welterweight
Men's welterweight
Men's middleweight
Men's light-heavyweight
Men's heavyweight
Men's super-heavyweight
Women's flyweight
Women's lightweight
Women's middleweight

Team GB's Nicola Adams (right) takes on Ukraine's Tetyana Kob in the quarter-finals on her way to retaining the women's flyweight title.

Boxing

Nicola Adams led the way with a second gold as Team GB's 12-strong boxing team defied some tough draws to emerge from the competition with a medal of each colour, achieving their medals target in the process.

Nicola Adams provided the headline act for another successful Olympic Games for the boxers as she was crowned Team GB's first double Olympic boxing gold medallist in 92 years in Rio. The 33-year-old shrugged off a testing draw in the women's flyweight division, defeating London 2012 finalist Ren Cancan en route to the final where victory over Sarah Ouhramoune of France took her back to the top of the podium.

It was a magnificent achievement for Adams, who had been crowned world champion for the first time earlier in 2016, and it may not be her last as she ponders whether to target Tokyo in 2020 and the prospect of becoming a three-time champion.

Adams was joined on the podium by London's super-heavyweight Joe Joyce, who won a fine silver medal after a narrow final defeat to reigning world champion Tony Yoka of France, and top prospect Joshua Buatsi, who exceeded expectations to take bronze in the light-heavyweight division.

Given the difficult nature of the qualifying process, Team GB had worked wonders to qualify a boxer for all but one of the 13 men's and women's Olympic categories, and went to Rio with a team bursting with both youth and experience. If hopes of matching the London 2012 medal haul of five were always going to be a little ambitious, there were certainly multiple medal prospects, although the draw on the opening day of competition underlined just how difficult winning any medal was going to be.

The resurgent Cubans and the rising central Asian states of Kazakhstan and Uzbekistan – who would end up with seven boxing medals in Rio – were all likely to offer the stiffest of challenges, and so it proved. In that context, Buatsi's achievement was perhaps the most remarkable. Having been on the elite Team GB squad for less than a

"I don't cry – I can't remember the last time I cried – so to shed a tear on that podium showed how much it meant to me."

Nicola Adams.

Left: On the podium, Adams wipes away a tear as the emotion of winning a second successive Olympic gold medal hits her.

Right: Joe Joyce (in blue) was unlucky to lose a narrow decision to world champion Tony Yoka in the super-heavyweight gold medal bout.

Above: Joyce was consoled at ringside by London 2012 gold medallist and subsequent IBF world champion Anthony Joshua.

Below: Nicola Adams had to get past a familiar foe in her women's flyweight semi-final, her London 2012 final opponent Ren Cancan of China.

year, the 23-year-old was one of the less-fancied members of the squad, especially as he was set to face veteran Uzbek boxer Elshod Rasulov in his second bout.

But having quickly dispatched Kennedy Katende of Uganda on his Olympic debut, Buatsi was undaunted by the prospect of taking on Rasulov and produced a stunning performance, flooring his opponent three times on his way to a stoppage win. Victory over Algeria's Abdelhafid Benchabla in his next bout ensured Buatsi a medal, but he was forced to settle for bronze when he came up against a strong Kazakh in Adilbek Niyazymbetov in his semi-final.

Joyce, meanwhile, was making predictably powerful progress as he sought to emulate his friend and occasional sparring partner Anthony Joshua, the London 2012 winner who subsequently went on to be crowned the IBF world heavyweight champion. Watched by Joshua at ringside, the unassuming Joyce thumped out his first three opponents with comparative ease to reach the final, but his aggressive work did not

impress the judges in the gold-medal match, who plumped instead for Yoka's accuracy and consigned Joyce to silver.

That brought the curtain down on a successful competition for performance director Rob McCracken, who nevertheless admitted an air of slight disappointment for squad members who had missed out on medals elsewhere. Youngster Galal Yafai kicked off the boxing competition with an easy win over Simplice Fotsala at light-flyweight and had nothing to be ashamed of in a subsequent defeat to accomplished Cuban Joahnys Argilagos.

Served with arguably the toughest draw of all, Birtley welterweight Pat McCormack looked excellent in defeating Kazakh boxer Ablaikhan Zhussupov in his first-round bout, before dropping a split decision to another Cuban, Yasniel Toledo. Josh Kelly and Antony Fowler were also beaten by Kazakhs – in Kelly's case, Daniyar Yeleussinov, the eventual winner – while heavyweight Lawrence Okolie fell to the vastly

experienced Cuban Erislandy Savon in his second fight.

Savannah Marshall, steeled by the desire to avoid a repeat of her first-round defeat in London, shrugged off the nerves with a fine first-round win over Anna Laurel of Sweden in the women's middleweight division. But Marshall, like so many of her teammates the recipient of a tough draw, narrowly lost her next bout to familiar foe Nouchka Fontijn of the Netherlands, who went on to take silver behind defending champion Claressa Shields of the US.

Joe Cordina of Wales, the reigning European champion, went into the competition with high hopes of a medal but was beaten in his second bout by Uzbek Hurshid Tojibaev, while both Qais Ashfaq and Muhammad Ali lost their opening contests.

Ultimately, from a spirited set of performances, it was Adams who once again emerged on top, the scale of her achievement in rising out of years in the shadows to become double Olympic champion apparent in the tears that fell during her crowning moment on the podium.

Buatsi impact

With one mighty right hand, London light-heavyweight Joshua Buatsi announced his name to the boxing world in Rio. The inexperienced Buatsi was given little chance in his bout against experienced Uzbek Elshod Rasulov, but he clattered his opponent to the canvas and repeated the feat twice more to score a third-round stoppage victory and ultimately went on to win a bronze medal for Team GB.

Potkonen proves point

It was a nightmare result for Ireland but Katie Taylor's first-round defeat to Finnish veteran Mira Potkonen in the women's lightweight division showed just how far the sport has evolved since it made its Olympic bow at London 2012. Then Taylor skated to gold, but in Rio the rising strength of the sport was encapsulated in the performance of Potkonen, who rose to the occasion to claim a wafer-thin split-decision win.

Opposite page: Team GB light-heavyweight Joshua Buatsi produced a big shock when he floored the experienced Uzbek boxer Elshod Rasulov three times on his way to a third-round stoppage victory.

Above left: Buatsi shows off his bronze medal, one of three collected as Team GB met their target.

Above: Heavyweight Lawrence Okolie was one of several British boxers to suffer from tough draws, when he came up against Cuban star Erislandy Savon in only his second bout.

Below: A first-round defeat for irish boxing icon Katie Taylor, against Mira Potkonen of Finland, proved the rapid rise in quality of women's boxing.

Canoeing

Lagoa Rodrigo de Freitas - in the shadow of Christ the Redeemer - was the stunning setting for the canoe sprint events while the canoe slalom took place at the Deodoro Olympic Whitewater Stadium.

Events

CANOE SLALOM
Men's C-1
Men's C-2
Men's & Women's K-1

CANOE SPRINT
Men's & Women's K-1 200m
Men's C-1 200m
Men's C-1 1,000m
Men's C-2 1,000m
Men's K-1 1,000m
Men's K-2 200m
Men's K-2 1,000m
Men's K-4 1,000m
Women's K-1 500m
Women's K-2 500m
Women's K-4 500m

Joe Clarke's Olympic gold medal was the first Team GB had ever won in the men's K1 canoe slalom discipline.

Canoe Slalom

Two medals, including a historic gold in the men's K1 canoe slalom, meant a successful Games for Team GB at the Whitewater Stadium in Deodoro.

Four years after Tim Baillie and Etienne Stott won Team GB's first canoe slalom gold medal, Joe Clarke delivered a second in Rio as Team GB returned with two medals from the slalom events. Clarke's K1 gold was followed up by David Florence and Richard Hounslow claiming silver in the C2 for the second Games running.

As a child, Clarke received a picture from five-time Olympic gold medallist Sir Steve Redgrave which was signed with the phrase "no stone unturned". It was advice heeded by the man from Staffordshire who, aged 23, secured Olympic gold at the first time of asking by winning the men's K1 canoe slalom.

Britain's Paul Ratcliffe (Sydney 2000) and Campbell Walsh (Athens 2004) had won silvers in the event but Clarke surpassed both with a podium-topping time of 88.53 seconds to become Team GB's first gold medallist in the event. "I left no stone unturned out there," Clarke said. "I nearly had to pinch myself to wake myself up. I thought it was a dream. To think it's real is, whoa, out of this world."

Florence and Hounslow added another medal by finishing second in the C2, just as they did at London 2012 behind countrymen Baillie and Stott. The duo were denied gold in Rio by Slovakian cousins Ladislav and Peter Skantar, who won gold with a searing final run to win by 0.43 seconds. It was a third silver medal for Florence, whose first came in Beijing in the C1.

In Rio, he missed out on a medal in the individual event as the reigning world champion never recovered from an early mistake and admitted he got the middle section "pretty catastrophically wrong" as he finished 10th and last in the final. But his recovery with Hounslow left the 34-year-old satisfied.

"I'm not disappointed at all," Florence said. "It wasn't quite gold, but after the disappointment in the C1, we just wanted to put together a really solid run and perform to the best of our ability. In a sport like this, when you spend all your time preparing and the slightest of mistakes costs you a medal, I'm really pleased with the way we held that run together."

"You can never take anything for granted in this sport and then I am actually standing on the podium and that national anthem is playing. To hear that was like 'wow'."

K1 canoe slalom gold medallist **Joe Clarke**.

Above: Joe Clarke makes a splash as he celebrates winning gold in the men's K1 canoe slalom event.

Opposite page: Clarke shows off his gold medal after winning the men's K1.

Left: David Florence (right) and Richard Hounslow collected silver medals for the second successive Games.

Below left: Fiona Pennie in action in the women's K1 semi-final.

Slovakia success

Slovakia have a proud history in the men's C2 and the Skantar cousins, Ladislav and Peter, produced a scintillating display to earn their country's fourth gold medal in five Olympic Games. Their success was perhaps understandable, having taken up the sport aged eight. "We come from a very small village and there were only two possibilities: play football or go for double canoeing," said Ladislav. Clearly they made the right choice.

Spain reign

Maialen Chourraut proved motherhood is no barrier to sporting success with victory in the women's K1. The Spaniard won bronze at London 2012 and then took time out of the sport to have a child, with her return to the Games exceeding her own expectations. "When I started paddling my coach, who is my husband now, taught our small team the importance of perseverance," she said. "I think this is the key."

Canoe Sprint

Liam Heath headed to Rio with one Olympic bronze to his name. He came back with a gold and a silver, as well as the title of Britain's most decorated Olympic canoeist.

It was in 2009 that Liam Heath decided to give canoeing another go after initially giving up the sport to focus on his degree at Loughborough University. Seven years later he was an Olympic champion after taking gold in the K1 200 metres at Rio's picturesque Lagoa.

Heath, who two days earlier had won silver with Jon Schofield in the K2 200m, swept past France's Maxime Beaumont in the closing stages to take victory by 0.17 seconds. After a quick check of the photo finish, the 32-year-old could start his celebrations. "I've got the set now, bronze in London, silver and gold here – it's incredible," he said. Victory made Heath Britain's most successful

Olympic canoeist ahead of Tim Brabants, whose collection was a gold and two bronzes.

But it could have been very different had Heath decided to stay away from the sport. "To think if I hadn't come back in I'd be missing out on this is quite scary to be honest," he admitted. "I came out of university twiddling my thumbs a little bit. Then the 200m was announced as an Olympic discipline and I've always been pretty nifty over 200m. I left where I was working and committed full-time, without funding initially, jumped straight in the K2 with Jon and first World Cup hit gold." His partnership with Schofield proved fruitful again in Rio.

After the pair won bronze in London, they improved to silver at the Lagoa. Spanish duo Saul Craviotto Rivero and Cristian Toro won gold by 0.29 seconds but Heath and Schofield secured second by edging an incredibly close finish as the next four teams ended within a mere 0.12 seconds of each other.

Schofield had to temper his celebrations slightly as Heath switched his focus to the individual event. Schofield admitted the night before Heath's K1 success he "came back a little bit late and got changed outside the bedroom and snuck in like a ninja". But after Heath secured his piece of history, the celebrations could properly start.

"The last Olympics I smashed these paddles in half. I was reminded before this race that they are too expensive to do that again."

K2 200m silver medallist
Jon Schofield.

Left: Heath and Schofield went one better than their bronze medal in London.

Kozak treble

Hungary's Danuta Kozak was the undoubted star in the canoe sprint, becoming the first female to win the K1, K2 and K4 at the same Games as she took her career tally of Olympic golds to five. A demanding programme resulted in her racing seven times during six days of competition but it did not stop her adding to the two golds she won at London 2012 and her silver from Beijing 2008.

Brendel defends title

All eyes were on defending champion Sebastian Brendel in the final of the C1 1000m and the firm favourite held off the challenge of Brazil's Isaquias Queiroz to become the first man to defend his Olympic title in this event since Josef Holecek in 1952. Brendel and Queiroz also went up against each other in the C2 final four days later when the German triumphed again, with Jan Vandrey.

Top: Liam Heath heads for glory in the men's K1 200m.

Above: Danuta Kozak's three golds took her overall tally to five.

Below: Heath and Jon Schofield celebrate after snatching silver in a blanket finish for second place in the K2 200m.

Cycling

The cycling took place across the city, from the stunning Fort Copacabana to the Team GB medal factory at the Rio Olympic Velodrome.

Events

BMX
Men's & Women's individual

MOUNTAIN BIKE
Men's & Women's cross-country

ROAD
Men's & Women's road race
Men's & Women's time trial

TRACK
Men's & Women's sprint
Men's & Women's team sprint
Men's & Women's keirin
Men's & Women's team pursuit
Men's & Women's omnium

The Team GB quartet on their way to gold and a new world record in the men's team pursuit at the velodrome.

BMX

Liam Phillips was one of the favourites for gold in the BMX only for his Games to come to a painful end with a crash in the first quarter-final. But he had defied the odds just to make it to Rio.

Having been an Olympic finalist in 2012, world champion in 2013 and World Cup series winner in 2014 and 2015, Liam Phillips went to Rio with all the pedigree needed to be a favourite in the BMX. But his Games proved frustrating from the off. He qualified in 10th position to land an unfavourable seeding in the three-race quarter-finals.

He was leading when he crashed with Latvia's Maris Strombergs and Switzerland's David Graf in the first bend of the opening race and was left to walk to the end, registering a 'did not finish' and finding himself eliminated from a competition which had barely begun.

The 27-year-old from Burnham-on-Sea suffered minor concussion but his pain was ultimately more mental than physical. Afterwards, he thanked coach Grant White, British Cycling's support staff and girlfriend Jess Varnish for enabling him to even make the start, revealing he had broken his collarbone two months before the Games and fought his way back to fitness.

It was news that put a different complexion on the results – it was remarkable he had been able to compete at all – but that did little

to ease his frustration. "I'm beyond devastated and will be for some time I'm sure," Phillips wrote on Twitter. "Sixty-two days ago I smashed my left collarbone into five pieces. With the help of an unbelievable group of people and some hard yards I got to the start gate in the best possible shape. It wasn't the fairy tale ending I'd hoped for, far from it, but that small group of people at least gave me the opportunity to give it a go."

Kyle Evans also missed out on the semi-finals, ending Team GB's participation in the men's event won by American Connor Fields.

"If I know Liam he'll bounce back in no time. He's an incredible athlete."

Teammate **Kyle Evans**.

Top: Mariana Pajon flies highest and furthest above a sea of Colombian supporters.

Above: Liam Phillips in action before his Olympics came to a sudden end.

Pajon's home help

World champion Mariana Pajon of Colombia was racing in her home continent and had plenty of support for the final of the women's race. She rewarded them with victory before raising her bike in the air and waving the Colombian flag. "This is better than anything," she said. "It's so beautiful. I feel like I was at home with so many Colombian fans in the grandstands."

Mountain Bike

Britain had one surprise entry in the cross-country mountain bike as Grant Ferguson was called into the squad in July and he relished the opportunity.

Grant Ferguson was a late inclusion in the squad and his selection for the men's mountain bike meant Team GB were represented across all four cycling disciplines. No Team GB cyclist had originally qualified but a reallocation of unused places opened the door and the 22-year-old from Peebles, fifth in the 2014 Commonwealth Games on home soil, was the lucky man to board the plane to Brazil.

Ferguson had been part of the BOA's Olympic Ambition Programme which allowed him some experience of London 2012 and that stood him in good stead for his debut. He started on the fifth row before gradually moving through the pack to finish a creditable 17th on a testing course made even more difficult by heavy overnight rain.

While Ferguson was in his first season as an elite rider in the sport, many of his fellow competitors were far more experienced. Slovakia's road world champion Peter Sagan opted to go back to his off-road roots and compete in the mountain bike. He worked his way up into the top five early on before being hampered by a flat tyre. Switzerland's Nino Schurter claimed gold to complete a long-awaited progress to the top step of the podium, having won bronze in Beijing and silver in London.

In the women's race, Sweden's Jenny Rissveds pulled clear on the first long climb of the last lap and ended a comfortable winner ahead of Maja Wloszczowska of Poland, who was also runner-up in Beijing eight years ago. Catharine Pendrel held off Canadian team-mate Emily Batty to claim the bronze medal.

Super Schurter

The relief was clear when Nino Schurter crossed the finish line and raised his arms aloft as he finally claimed Olympic gold in the men's mountain bike at the third time of asking. He pulled clear on the sixth lap to complete his medal collection and said: "If I look back, I needed silver in London to get back and be strong here. For me, it is the perfect story."

Above: Swedish rider Jenny Rissveds on her way to victory in the women's cross-country mountain bike.

Right: Grant Ferguson's Olympic debut was a proud occasion, and he acquitted himself well despite being unable to finish on the podium.

53

Road Cycling

With a three-time Tour de France winner and reigning women's world champion in their ranks, Britain had hopes of snatching glory amid the tumult of the road races and more structured time trials.

Team GB's track dominance is hard to replicate on the road, where the element of chance is greater, but the men's team could not have arrived in better shape.

Each member of the five-strong squad had experienced individual or team success in the Tour de France – nobody more than Chris Froome, who had just joined the elite club of eight riders with three or more Tour wins.

Team GB played their cards creatively in the mountainous 237.5km men's road race, but it became clear Froome was not the ace in their pack. Instead it was Geraint Thomas who stayed with the leaders over the final climb.

A crash for Italian favourite Vincenzo Nibali on the final descent left it wide open, but, when Thomas also hit the deck, Britain's medal hopes were left by the roadside as Belgian Greg Van Avermaet chased down Rafal Majka and took gold.

On the road, the 137km women's race played out in similar fashion to the men's as it was defined by a late crash, a horrific fall taking out leader Annemiek van Vleuten and allowing fellow Dutchwoman Anna van der Breggen to claim gold. Behind the drama, Armitstead finished fifth.

Attention turned to the time trials, where Froome was hoping to emulate Sir Bradley Wiggins's famous Tour de France and Olympic Games double of 2012.

But, although the course suited him, the exertions of a long season perhaps caught up with him only 17 days after the Tour ended in Paris.

Swiss veteran Fabian Cancellara rolled back the years to claim gold ahead of Dutch time-trial specialist Tom Dumoulin over the 54.5km course, with Froome taking bronze, repeating his third place in London four years earlier. Thomas, handed a surprise place in the time trial after withdrawals, finished ninth after a fine ride in a discipline which is not his strong suit.

The women's time trial was won by American veteran Kristin Armstrong, 42, as Team GB's Emma Pooley had to settle for 14th place after being tempted out of retirement by the hilly nature of the 29.8km course.

"It's been an amazing summer. The Tour was the big target for me. To come here and to try to back it up and to come away with a medal is really special."

Chris Froome.

Happy tears

When Kristin Armstrong won a third straight women's time trial the day before her 43rd birthday, her five-year-old son was puzzled by her tears. "Mama, why are you crying?" asked Lucas as he ran to meet her. "You won!" He was told they were tears of joy after the American proved age is no barrier as the oldest cyclist in the field by seven years.

Fab farewell

Fabian Cancellara could have been forgiven for thinking he would never again experience the high of being on top of the world. The 35-year-old Swiss, who claimed time-trial gold at Beijing in 2008 and won the last of his four world titles in 2010, was in his final season but returned to his best as he finished 47 seconds clear to secure a farewell gold.

Top: Team GB are set to lead from the front at the start of the Olympic men's road race.

Above: Swiss legend Fabian Cancellara heads for the men's time trial gold medal.

Opposite page: Chris Froome had to be content with time trial bronze for the second successive Olympics.

Right: Kristin Armstrong's third gold came at the age of 42.

Track Cycling

Team GB's cyclists travelled to Rio well-prepared and ended the track programme in a familiar position at the top of the velodrome medal table with more golds than the rest of the world combined.

This was supposed to be the Olympic Games when the rest of the world caught up, but the velodrome once again belonged to Team GB.

Six gold medals, four silvers and one bronze were won at the velodrome as British cyclists, just as they had in London, dominated. The Netherlands were next best with two medals, one gold and one silver.

Britain had won seven out of ten titles at the previous two Olympic Games. Surely the rest of the world had worked out by now how to take some medals off Britain?

It soon became apparent that this was not the case. It started with the men's team sprint as a third straight Olympic title was won, despite not claiming a world crown since 2005. Britain's three-man, three-lap squad have a habit of peaking every four years and did so again as Jason Kenny, Phil Hindes and Callum Skinner claimed gold in 42.440 seconds, an Olympic record. New Zealand's Ethan Mitchell, Sam Webster and Ed Dawkins, the world champions, had to settle for silver and France bronze.

Then came the men's team pursuit as Sir Bradley Wiggins won his fifth Olympic gold and a British record eighth medal in all. Ed Clancy, Steven Burke, Owain Doull and Wiggins beat their own world record

in the four-man, four-kilometres event – set in the first round 80 minutes earlier – to win gold in three minutes 50.265 seconds. Australia had advanced to the final while keeping Jack Bobridge in reserve, having so far not shown their full hand, and led until two laps to go when an almighty roar erupted, with Britain edging in front for the first time. With Burke already dropped, Wiggins led Clancy and Doull to the line to win by 0.743 seconds.

A day after the men's success, there was a victory in the corresponding women's event thanks to Laura Trott, Joanna Rowsell-Shand, Elinor Barker and Katie Archibald. Britain clocked a world record in qualifying and the semi-final, their second mark of 4:12.152 beating the previous best the USA had set moments earlier in their own semi-final. Britain stuck with the same quartet throughout, leaving Ciara Horne in reserve.

"He's a quiet guy, but he's surely one of the most talented athletes we've produced in any sport, no question."

British Cycling head coach **Iain Dyer** on Jason Kenny.

Left: Philip Hindes, Jason Kenny and Callum Skinner power to victory in a tight men's team sprint final.

Opposite: Golden couple Laura Trott and Jason Kenny.

Above: Sir Bradley Wiggins (right) celebrates his fifth and final Olympic gold medal, alongside teammates (from left) Steven Burke, Owain Doull and Ed Clancy.

Below: Team GB's women pursuit team broke the world record not once, but three times. The determination is clear to see during their race against Canada.

Rio 2016

USA's Sarah Hammer, Kelly Catlin, Chloe Dygert and Jennifer Valente made the early running, but Britain overtook them after 1,625m and surged onwards to a phenomenal win.

Just 17 minutes later, the medal tally increased further when Becky James added keirin silver with a stunning last lap. James had been beset by illness and injury since her double world title win in Minsk 2013, suffering a cancer scare and a knee injury that left her unable to ride a bike for fourth months.

The 24-year-old from Abergavenny began the last lap of the final in sixth and last place. She followed the instruction of coach Jan van Eijden to go round high up the outside and powered round the final bend and into the medal positions to finish behind Dutch cyclist Elis Ligtlee.

The final of the men's sprint was an all-British affair and it was Kenny who came out on top with a 2-0 win against teammate and room-mate Skinner. That was his fifth Olympic gold, but he was not done yet as he emulated Sir Chris Hoy's achievement of three gold medals at one Games and a total of six golds and one silver.

The 28-year-old from Bolton's sixth gold came in the keirin, having kept his cool in the final medal race on the track. He survived a scare when the race was paused as officials studied footage to determine if he had illegally overtaken the motorised Derny bike before it had left the track.

British Cycling head coach Iain Dyer spoke to the race officials during the lengthy delay and discovered they did not have a camera at the point where the Derny leaves the track, so he offered footage gathered by British Cycling's performance analysts, Will Forbes and Dr Debs Sides, from in line with the incident. Fortunately the officials were prepared to accept the assistance and Kenny was cleared to continue.

The restart was also paused – with all six riders again starting – and at the third time of asking no-one could live with Kenny's blistering pace.

Above: Laura Trott celebrates after winning the omnium gold medal.

Opposite top: Becky James in action on her way to silver in the women's Keirin.

Opposite bottom: Inside Rio's velodrome.

It proved to be a dream night for Team GB's 'golden couple' as Kenny's fiancée Trott won her second gold of the Games.

The 24-year-old from Cheshunt took a commanding 24-point advantage into the points race, which concluded the six-discipline omnium, and rode a masterful race to defend the title she won at London 2012 and take her to four career Olympic gold medals, the most for a female British Olympian.

Further to the success of Trott and Kenny, there was also a second silver medal of the Games for James in the women's sprint and a bronze for Katy Marchant. James reached the final but missed out on gold as multiple world champion Kristina Vogel of Germany claimed a 2-0 win while Marchant beat Ligtlee 2-0 in the race

for third.

Every member of the British track team to compete in Rio won a medal, even Mark Cavendish, who snagged the prize he has coveted for so long with silver in the omnium. After eight years of trying and at the third time of asking, Cavendish finished behind Italy's Elia Viviani while defending champion Lasse Norman Hansen of Denmark took bronze. The Manxman went into the concluding points race with a 16-point deficit. Twenty points were available for gaining a lap, but Cavendish was heavily marked and Viviani's advantage was too much to bridge.

Instead, Cavendish had to fend off attacks from riders vying to depose him from the podium, steadily accumulating points in the sprints which came every 10 laps to take silver. While it was not the gold medal he had hoped for, it was another fantastic achievement in a stunning career, especially as it came only a month after taking his tally of Tour de France stage wins to 30, second on the all-time list to

Eddy Merckx's 34.

"I'm always going to be a marked man and I decided halfway that I couldn't get a lap; no-one was going to let me get a lap," said Cavendish. "I'd just have to pick off sprints one by one. Ultimately I couldn't have done any more. I have to be happy."

The same could not be said of the other nations, who were left scratching their heads as Team GB peaked for a third straight Olympic Games. British Cycling head coach Iain Dyer said: "A lot has been said about the culture of this programme this year. I have to say – and I think this backs it up – that our culture is one of success.

"Someone asked me how many medals we'd won and I didn't really know. We knew that we were timing it right for where we were at, we just didn't know what the outcome of that would be in terms of where the rest of the world would be. It's proved it was extremely successful. Hopefully it inspires a younger generation to come and we'll see them in the fullness of time."

Left: Team GB teammates Becky James (right) and Katy Marchant took silver and bronze respectively in the women's sprint.

Below: Mark Cavendish earned a long-awaited Olympic medal as he took silver in the men's omnium.

Right: Sealed with a kiss, Jason Kenny and Laura Trott will never forget when they struck gold within 90 minutes of each other.

Below right: Sir Bradley Wiggins acknowledges the fantastic crowd support after winning his fifth gold medal.

For the record

World Records
Cycling – Track: Women's team sprint
China (31.928s)

Cycling – Track: Men's team pursuit
Great Britain (3:50.265s)

Cycling – Track: Women's team pursuit
Great Britain (4:10.236s)

Olympic Records
Cycling – Track: Men's team sprint
Great Britain (42.440s)

Cycling – Track: Men's sprint
Jason Kenny (Great Britain) 9.551s

Cycling – Track: Women's sprint
Becky James (Great Britain) 10.721s

Cycling – Track: Men's omnium
Lasse Norman Hansen (Denmark)
4:14.982s

Sealed with a kiss
Jason Kenny did not have to wait long to celebrate his victory in the Keirin with his loved one. Fiancée Laura Trott had earlier won omnium gold and then watched nervously before bursting into tears as Kenny added to their medal collection. They shared a kiss on the track to the delight of the crowd and Kenny admitted: "I couldn't understand a word she was saying. She was bawling her eyes out."

Worth the wait
China had been agonisingly relegated to second place in the women's team sprint at London 2012 for an illegal lane change so their success in Rio was well overdue. Gong Jinje, now riding with Zhong Tianshi, had her celebrations cruelly cut short four years ago but was not to be denied after victory over Russia in the final, with the duo having already broken the world record in the first round.

Equestrian

The Olympic Equestrian Centre in Deodoro hosted the showjumping and dressage arena as well as the cross-country course.

Events

DRESSAGE
Team dressage
Individual dressage

EVENTING
Team eventing
Individual eventing

SHOWJUMPING
Team showjumping
Individual showjumping

Nick Skelton on his way to winning individual showjumping gold.

Dressage

The awe-inspiring Charlotte Dujardin defended her gold medal from London 2012, while also spearheading a strong Team GB performance in the team event to come away with two medals from two events.

The opening day of dressage competition in Rio saw British debutants Spencer Wilton and Fiona Bigwood start their Olympic campaigns. The defending team champions sat third at the end of the first day, with Wilton producing a score of 72.686 per cent on Super Nova II and Bigwood scoring 77.157 on Orthilia.

Britain continued to impress on the second day, with two stars of their team triumph in 2012 returning to the Olympic arena. After Carl Hester had posted a score of 75.529 on Nip Tuck, Charlotte Dujardin and Valegro delivered a stunning display on their way to scoring 85.071. Britain finished the day in second with a score of 79.252 while Dujardin sat top of the individual rankings.

Dujardin led from the front once again in Friday's team finale, scoring 82.983 as Britain's team clinched a sensational silver medal with a score of 78.595. Hester was thrilled with the result and said: "We are very happy. Any medal, we would have been very happy with because any Olympic Games produces a lot of nerves, different atmospheres and different rides."

As well as securing a silver medal, Dujardin, Hester and Bigwood all qualified for the individual final on the back of their performances in the team event. Both Bigwood and Hester put in strong performances in the final, posting scores of 76.018 and 82.553 respectively, but the stars of the show were undoubtedly Dujardin and Valegro. The defending champions obliterated the field, producing an Olympic record grand prix freestyle score of 93.857 per cent to take gold.

"Coming here, I had to defend that title, I had expectation, I had the pressure and I did feel it a little bit for the first time."

Charlotte Dujardin.

After becoming only the second British woman to win three Olympic gold medals, Dujardin said: "I knew it could be one of the last times with Valegro. I know I am not going to do another Olympics with him. But as soon as I got into the arena, Valegro gave me this most amazing feeling and it put a smile on my face. I knew I was fine. I owe it to him to finish at the top and I've done it. I am going to make sure it happens again (on another horse) but he is a once-in-a-lifetime horse."

Above: Team silver medallists, from left, Fiona Bigwood, Charlotte Dujardin, Carl Hester and Spencer Wilton.

Top right: Valegro gets a final outing in the Olympic spotlight with Charlotte Dujardin.

Right: Charlotte Dujardin shows off her gold medal after successfully defending her individual dressage title.

Far right: Hester riding Nip Tuck.

Eventing

Britain's eventers produced strong performances in the dressage and showjumping but a disappointing day in the cross-country saw them miss out on an Olympic team medal for the first time since Atlanta 20 years ago.

The eventing began with two days of dressage on the opening weekend of the Games before Monday's cross-country test and the showjumping finale on day four. Britain got off to a dream start, with former world number one William Fox-Pitt producing a dressage score of 37.0 penalties on Chilli Morning to lead after the first day. Gemma Tattersall was Britain's other rider on day one and posted a score of 47.2 aboard Quicklook V.

Fox-Pitt, 47, who was placed in an induced coma only 10 months earlier after a cross-country fall left him seriously injured, was thrilled with his start. "That was what I was dreaming of," he said. "Chilli is great on the flat, and he did very good tests at the Caen 2014 World Equestrian Games and Malmo 2013 European Championships, and I did not want to let him down."

Fox-Pitt remained on top after day two, with Pippa Funnell on Billy The Biz in 16th with a score of 43.9. Kitty King, the last member of Team GB to go, was in joint 26th after producing a score of 46.80 while Tattersall's opening-day score saw her sit 32nd. But Britain's medal hopes were dealt a huge blow on day three when Fox-Pitt collected 20 penalties as a result of a cross-country run-out with Chilli Morning. With Tattersall having two run-outs, Funnell running out at the final water challenge and King having a refusal on Ceylor LAN, Britain were 91 penalties off third place with just the showjumping remaining.

Although Britain's combinations enjoyed success on day four, with Funnell, Fox-Pitt and King all going clear, they could only manage a fifth-place finish as France took gold, with Germany second and Australia third. Meanwhile, Fox-Pitt came 12th in the individual standings as Germany's Michael Jung claimed gold.

Fox-Pitt was pleased to finish the competition on a high and said: "It was really great to finish on a good note after the disappointment of Monday. With a bit more luck, we would have been up there. We just didn't have that luck with us."

"It is very exciting for the future with the young horses we have in what is a very strong team. Maybe it is going to be Tokyo 2020 for us. I keep on dreaming."

William Fox-Pitt.

Above: William Fox-Pitt in cross-country action on Chilli Morning.

Right: A relaxed Team GB pre-Olympic Games, from left, William Fox-Pitt, Pippa Funnell, Gemma Tattershall and Kitty King.

Opposite page: Quicklook V is a handful for Gemma Tattersall.

Jung again

Germany's Michael Jung retained his Olympic eventing title despite having to ride his second-choice horse. His original ride Takinou contracted an infection in July so 16-year-old gelding Sam FBW was taken instead and Jung triumphed by a margin of 7.1 penalties from France's Astier Nicolas to become the first rider since New Zealand's Mark Todd in Seoul 28 years ago to win successive individual golds.

Showjumping

Veteran Nick Skelton provided one of the stories of the Olympic Games when he claimed the individual showjumping crown to become the oldest winner of an equestrian gold medal.

Expectations were sky high as Team GB's showjumpers entered the Olympic Arena with the aim of building on their achievements in London. Although they could not defend the team title they won in 2012, a historic gold was secured on the final day of equestrian competition. Nick Skelton, 58, overcame adversity and serious injury – a broken neck 16 years ago, persistent chronic back pain and a hip replacement – to win individual gold on Big Star.

The showjumping began on day nine of the Games with Britain's team, including two members from London 2012, Skelton and Ben Maher, as well as brothers John and Michael Whitaker, all in action in the prelude to the team and individual competitions. The quartet, who have notched up more than 20 Olympic Games appearances between them, made a solid start, with veteran John Whitaker leading their charge on the first day of competition.

The 61-year-old produced a superb clear round on Ornellaia after Skelton, Maher and Michael Whitaker had each finished on four penalties. Things did not go quite as smoothly in the first round, however. With only eight places available in Wednesday's second round, Britain missed out after finishing 12th with a total score of 13 penalties on Tuesday.

"I was just emotional on the podium because I am so happy with what I've done. To do it now is unbelievable. It is pretty emotional for all concerned."

Nick Skelton.

Golden Oldie

Nick Skelton battled to hold back the tears on the podium after showing nerves of steel to win Team GB's first individual Olympic showjumping gold. Skelton and Big Star set a scorching pace of 42.82 seconds in the jump-off, despite being first to go, and no other rider could match it. The 58-year-old said: "He is the best horse I am ever likely to have."

But Skelton and Maher moved through to the next individual phase before going on to book spots in Friday's final, along with 33 others. Michael Whitaker had also qualified for the third individual round but had to withdraw after his horse, Cassionato, showed colic symptoms.

In the final, Skelton, competing in his seventh Olympic Games, clinched Britain's first individual showjumping Olympic gold medal following a six-way jump-off. After posting double clear rounds, Warwickshire-based Skelton and Big Star, who were first to go in the jump-off, set a phenomenal pace of 42.82 which none of their rivals came close to matching. Skelton finished more than half a second quicker than Sweden's Peder Fredricson in second.

Following his victory, Skelton said: "I have been in the sport a long time.

I am so happy – it was amazing. That jump-off has been the biggest nerves of the Games for me."

Above: Nick Skelton in action in the gold medal jump-off.

Opposite page: Skelton stands atop the medal podium.

Below: Ben Maher in action aboard Tic Tac.

Fencing

Carioca Arena 3 was the venue for the fencing at Rio 2016 – featuring three individual and two team events for both men and women – before being turned into a specialist sports school with capacity for 850 full-time students.

Events

Men's & Women's individual epee
Men's & Women's team epee
Men's & Women's individual foil
Men's team foil
Men's individual sabre
Women's individual sabre
Women's team sabre

Team GB's Richard Kruse celebrates beating former double Olympic champion Andrea Cassara of Italy in the last 16.

Fencing

Team GB came so close in their bid for a first Olympic fencing medal since 1964, with Richard Kruse only one win away after producing one of the finest performances from a Team GB fencer in history.

Richard Kruse headed to Rio boasting a best Olympic finish of eighth from three Games – and that was on his debut in Athens 12 years earlier. He travelled to South America more in hope than expectation of a medal, yet the 33-year-old Londoner defied even his own expectations with a series of superb performances, only to fall agonisingly short in his podium push as he was narrowly beaten to bronze by Timur Safin of Russia.

Kruse's scalps included former double Olympic champion Andrea Cassara of Italy in the last 16 but, after dropping his semi-final tie against American world number one Alexander Massialas, Kruse left himself too much to do against Safin, when victory would have made him Britain's first Olympic Games fencing medallist in 52 years.

Not since Bill Hoskyns took silver in the men's epee in Tokyo 1964 has a British fencer made it on to an Olympic podium. Trailing 12-5 in their first-to-15 encounter, Kruse launched a spectacular comeback which plainly won the support of the capacity crowd, hauling back to within a single point of the Russian before succumbing to the crucial final hit and losing 15-13.

Kruse said afterwards: "I didn't know it would have been our first medal of the Games, but I knew it would have been the first in fencing for many years. I couldn't quite convert it but it's all a bit of fun – we travel the world playing the sport we love and I've beaten some good people here."

Safin had beaten Kruse's teammate, British number one James Davis, 15-13 in the last 16 while the third British competitor, Laurence

"It's all a bit of fun – we travel the world playing the sport we love."

Richard Kruse.

Halsted, lost his opening bout to China's Chen Haiwei.

Kruse's initial conqueror, the gold medal favourite Massialas, eventually had to settle for the silver medal after being beaten 15-11 in the final by Daniele Garozzo of Italy. Kruse's bid for a medal in the team event, for which Britain qualified by winning gold at the inaugural

Historic hijab

Winning bronze in the women's team sabre, Ibtihaj Muhammad made history in Rio as the first American woman to compete at the Olympic Games wearing a hijab. The 30-year-old said: "I'm hoping that through my experiences here at the Olympic Games – winning a medal – that I combat those stereotypes about Muslims and African Americans and even women."

Underdog strikes

Yana Egorian described compatriot Sofia Velikaya as her "role model" and was the underdog in the women's sabre final, but it was the younger Russian who claimed gold on her Olympic debut. A tense contest went down to the wire but Egorian levelled the scores at 14-14 before landing one more hit to condemn Velikaya to a second successive silver medal, having also been runner-up at London 2012.

European Games in Baku last year, was also foiled by defeat to Russia in the quarter-finals. Britain's team of four, which also included Marcus Mepstead, ended up sixth.

Opposite page: Great Britain's Richard Kruse celebrates after beating USA's Gerek Meinhardt.

Above: Kruse on his way to victory over Algeria's Hamid Sintes (left) in the men's foil competition.

Top left: Bronze medallist Ibtihaj Muhammad was the first American to compete at the Games in a hijab.

Golf

Golf made an historic return to the Olympic Games after a 112-year absence, on a purpose-built course on Rio's Reserva de Marapendi, where men and women competed across four rounds.

Events

Men's individual
Women's individual

Justin Rose celebrates an historic gold medal for Team GB in the men's golf.

Golf

Golf was back in the Olympic Games for the first time in more than a century and major winners Justin Rose and Henrik Stenson produced a brilliant battle which went all the way to the final hole.

Golf's Olympic return after 112 years ended in thrilling fashion with Team GB's Justin Rose pipping Henrik Stenson of Sweden to gold on the 18th green. Rose had been an outstanding ambassador for golf in the Olympics and the former US Open winner arrived early to take part in the Opening Ceremony and sample some of the other sports.

Rose began an exhilarating final round a shot clear but Stenson's sensational closing 63 to capture The Open at Troon a month earlier highlighted the threat he posed.

The pair had teamed up to take three points out of three at the 2014 Ryder Cup and the quality of their golf was no less exceptional as they went head-to-head at Reserva de Marapendi. The contest was only settled at the 72nd hole, Rose pitching to three feet to set up a decisive birdie and Stenson failing to convert his long-range attempt.

Rose's closing 67 gave him a 16-under-par total, with silver the least Stenson deserved and fast-finishing American Matt Kuchar taking bronze.

"It feels absolutely incredible," Rose said afterwards. "I was on that last green, just sort of pinching myself and taking myself back to the quote that I had given about the Olympics all along: 'I hope my resumé one day reads multiple major champion and Olympic gold medallist'. I've been so up for it. I've been just so determined to represent Team GB as best as I could and it was just the most magical week, it really was."

While Masters champion Danny Willett shot a final-round 74 to finish on level par for the tournament, he said mixing with the other members of Team GB had been a pleasant experience. Willett said: "I had breakfast with Andy Murray and Jess Ennis-Hill and that's stuff you don't normally get to do."

In the women's event, South Korea's Inbee Park defied not having played since April to claim gold after a closing 66 saw her finish five clear of New Zealand's Lydia Ko, with China's Shanshan Feng third.

Team GB's Charley Hull finished tied for seventh and said: "My first Olympics was a fantastic experience and I got a good buzz off it. It is a shame I couldn't come away with a medal but I finished tied 7th. If you finish in the top 10 in a major it is a pretty good week so I am happy."

Teammate Catriona Matthew finished 29th overall after being level par for the tournament. After finishing one under in the final round, she said: "It was nice to finish with a good round. It has been great being at the Olympics. I have loved it."

"This is a dream come true. I've been thinking about Rio for a long, long time. I made it a big deal in my year."

Justin Rose.

Above: The first men's Olympic medallists for 112 years: Justin Rose, Henrik Stenson and Matt Kuchar.

Opposite above right: Eventual winner Rose plays out of a bunker on the second hole at Reserva de Marapendi.

Opposite right: Charley Hull finished seventh in the women's event, which she described as a 'fantastic experience'.

Rose blooms

Team GB's Justin Rose ensured golf returned to the Olympic Games in spectacular fashion with a hole-in-one on the first day of competition. Rose holed out from 191 yards on the fourth for what is believed to be the first ace in Olympic history. "It was one of those nice moments," said Rose. "When you are the first to do something, no-one can take it away from you."

Aces in spades

The third round of the women's competition produced two holes-in-one as the 140-yard eighth hole provided easy pickings for some. China's Xiya Lun was the first to find the cup from the tee and she was later followed by 19-year-old New Zealander Lydia Ko, although the Kiwi world number one eventually had to settle for the silver medal as South Korea's Inbee Park stormed to victory by five shots.

Gymnastics

All three gymnastics disciplines – artistic, rhythmic and trampoline – were staged at the Rio Olympic Arena in the region of Barra da Tijuca. This 15,000-seater indoor multi-purpose arena was first used at the 2007 Pan American Games and now was to see Max Whitlock lead Team GB to seven medals in total.

Events

ARTISTIC
Men's & Women's floor exercise
Men's & Women's individual all-around
Men's & Women's team all-around
Men's & Women's vault
Men's horizontal bar
Men's parallel bars
Men's pommel horse
Men's rings
Women's beam
Women's uneven bars

RHYTHMIC
Women's individual all-around
Women's team all-around

TRAMPOLINE
Men's & Women's individual

Max Whitlock on his way to his first gold medal of the Games on the pommel, one of two golds and a bronze the Team GB star collected in Rio.

Artistic

Team GB's gymnasts completed a fantastic resurgence in Brazil as they confounded expectations by claiming a remarkable seven medals to finish third in the overall gymnastics medal table behind USA and Russia.

British Gymnastics shone under the Team GB banner as they surpassed the four medals won in London 2012 with a magnificent seven in Rio. After making history by winning the men's individual all-around bronze, Max Whitlock broke more British records as he impressed with double gold success on the floor and pommel horse – where Louis Smith clinched silver – either side of Bryony Page's unexpected silver trampolining medal.

On the final day of gymnastics action, 16-year-old Amy Tinkler came home with bronze in the women's floor before Nile Wilson left British gymnastics in seventh heaven with bronze in the men's horizontal bar. British Gymnastics technical director Eddie Van Hoof summed up what the rest of the nation was thinking after clinching the seven-medal haul when he said: "It's beyond all dreams really – it's like you wake up and they all came true at once."

The success for British Gymnastics was all the more incredible given its parlous state only 12 years ago, when a series of below-par performances resulted in it temporarily losing all of its funding. Let us take you on a journey. Time travel with us back to the 1908 Games in London and watch a certain Walter Tysall of Birmingham claim silver with Team GB's last

"I still feel I can improve on my floor and my pommel. It's always been my dream to get my own move on the pommel horse and that will take a long time. Now I've got time on my side."

Double gold medallist **Max Whitlock**.

Left: Amy Tinkler, the youngest member Team GB member in Rio, took bronze in the women's floor final.

Below: Louis Smith in action in the final of the pommel competition.

Above: Team GB's women gymnasts, from left, Amy Tinkler, Rebecca Downie, Claudia Fragapane, Ruby Harrold and Ellie Downie.

Opposite page: Max Whitlock on his way to bronze in the individual all-around.

individual men's all-around gymnastics medal. Now, let's jump forward to over a century later to the Rio 2016 Olympic Games and see Whitlock inspire the nation as his performance earns bronze for Team GB in Rio.

On filling that 108-year void and taking bronze, Whitlock bowed to the greatness of all-conquering Japanese superstar Kohei Uchimura, who retained his title and extended his eight-year winning streak after edging past Ukraine's Oleg Verniaiev on the final piece of apparatus. For Whitlock, who had already won bronze medals in the team and pommel horse competitions at London 2012, a podium finish in the most prestigious gymnastics discipline proved the culmination of his rise to the top.

The 23-year-old from Hertfordshire had gone to Rio as a hot favourite to end Team GB's gymnastics gold drought, having been crowned Team GB's first men's individual world champion the previous year. Just four days later Whitlock made history by doing just that as he produced a flawless routine on the floor, coupled with mistakes by his major rivals, which saw him top the podium on a raucous night.

Whitlock scored 15.633 and beat two Brazilians, Diego Hypolito and Arthur Mariano, into second and third. The Brit was cheered on to the podium to collect his historic gold while the Brazilian pair milked the acclaim of the crowd. After a brief pose for photographers, Whitlock was ushered away to prepare for the pommel and came back refreshed and ready for more.

Less than two hours after clinching the floor gold, Whitlock found himself in the extraordinary position of being a double Olympic gold medallist after edging an emotional Smith into second place in a thrilling finish

to the pommel horse final. Starting fifth of eight finalists, Smith led the way with a score of 15.833 until Whitlock eclipsed him with 15.966 with one more athlete to go. When Russian Nikolai Kuksenkov could only manage an unspectacular routine to score 15.233, gold and silver for Whitlock and Smith were assured with America's Alexander Naddour bagging bronze. The pair embraced before being led out for their medal ceremony on a historic day for Team GB. Whitlock's feat was all the more remarkable for the fact he had to recover from a bout of glandular fever after becoming Britain's first male individual world champion in Glasgow, the illness making him doubtful to compete.

The doubts were not entirely assuaged by Whitlock's performance in the men's team final, where he was joined by Smith, Wilson, Brinn Bevan and Kristian Thomas, as Team GB narrowly missed out on a medal. The women's team, which consisted of Claudia Fragapane, Tinkler, Ruby Harrold, Ellie Downie and Becky Downie, came home fifth in their final.

There were bronzes to come for teenager Tinkler and Wilson. If Whitlock's success provided the headline act, Tinkler also bounced back from a disappointing series of qualifying results for the British women by winning an unexpected bronze in the women's floor final. At 16, the youngest member of the entire GB delegation, Tinkler held her nerve to reach the podium behind two Americans, including all-conquering gold medallist Simone Biles.

Moments later the impressive Wilson emulated his teammate by claiming bronze in a dramatic high bar final which saw defending champion Epke Zonderland of the Netherlands crash out.

Top: Nile Wilson celebrates his bronze medal finish in the men's high bar.

Above: Team GB's Rebecca Downie in action on the beam.

Opposite page: The scene in the Rio Olympic Arena during the gymnastic competition.

"It's beyond all dreams really – it's like you wake up and they all came true at once."

British Gymnastics technical director **Eddie Van Hoof**.

To the Max

Max Whitlock won the nation's first gymnastics gold in the men's floor event and followed it less than two hours later when he pipped teammate Louis Smith in the pommel horse. Whitlock had already claimed a historic bronze in the men's all-around behind his Japanese idol Kohei Uchimura and there were bronzes to come for Amy Tinkler and Nile Wilson and an unexpected silver medal for trampolinist Bryony Page.

Brilliant Biles

Until the Rio Games, Russia had won every gold medal in the sport since Sydney 2000 but were pipped to the top of the table this time around by a dominant USA team, who claimed four gymnastics golds from their 12-medal haul, all four from Simone Biles. The 19-year-old superstar triumphed in the vault, the team all-around, the floor exercise and the individual all-around while she also claimed a bronze medal in the beam.

Above: United States star Simone Biles was the Games' outstanding gymnast, collecting a haul of four gold medals and a bronze.

Opposite page: Bryony Page took a surprise silver medal in the trampolining.

Below: Men's all-around gold medallist Kohei Uchimura.

Trampoline

To cap a remarkable week for Team GB, Bryony Page clinched an unexpected gymnastics medal in the women's trampoline with silver.

Bryony Page earned the nation's first Olympic medal in trampolining while teammate Kat Driscoll, who was rated the better of the two medal chances, was placed a credible sixth. The 25-year-old Page, who finished 10th at the 2015 world championship in Odense, Denmark, scored 56.040 from her routine to finish runner-up behind Rosannagh MacLennan. The Canadian compiled a score of 56.465 to bag the gold medal while world champion Lin Dan of China sealed the final podium place with 55.885.

Page said: "I didn't expect to medal and to get a silver I couldn't have asked for more. I got up there and did my absolute best on that trampoline when it mattered in the final. I think once I've retired from the sport is when it will properly sink in. It's been an incredible journey so far and hopefully there is more to come."

A British woman had never before reached the final of the event, which made its Olympic debut in 2000, but Page qualified in seventh, with the top eight progressing, while compatriot Driscoll finished two places higher. Driscoll, who won world titles in the synchro and team events in 2013, had to settle for a sixth-place finish in the final with a score of 53.645. She said: "It's a real mix of emotions. We haven't had a girl make the final yet, so for two of us to do it is amazing. I'm so happy and proud to have just made the final."

Nathan Bailey's score of 106.795 in qualifying for the men's trampoline placed him ninth and saw him narrowly miss out on a spot in the final, which 2014 European champion Uladzislau Hancharou of Belarus went on to win ahead of Chinese duo Dong Dong and Gao Lei. Bailey said: "I don't think I've got a word that truly sums up what it's like out there. To be in such a competitive field for my first Games, it was just an amazing experience."

There was no British interest in the rhythmic gymnastics in Rio, where Russia dominated the finals as Margarita Mamun and Yana Kudryavtseva took gold and silver respectively ahead of third-placed Ganna Rizatdinova of Ukraine in the women's individual all-around. The Russians also claimed top spot on the podium ahead of Spain and Bulgaria in the women's team all-around competition.

"Just getting into the Olympic final, going out the back and doing our warm-up, I was like 'I'm an Olympic finalist!' Then when I found out I got the silver I was just so shell-shocked, it's just absolutely incredible."

Bryony Page.

Hockey

The men's and women's tournaments were staged at the Olympic Hockey Centre at Deodoro, a purpose-built venue that will now become home to Brazil's national teams.

Events

Men's
Women's

Team GB players celebrate their historic victory after beating the Netherlands in the gold medal match of the women's hockey.

Hockey

Team GB's women made history with a first hockey gold medal – and the first by any British team since the 1988 men's competition.

Video footage of Team GB's raucous flight home from Rio, with the women's hockey team leading the celebrations, was an enjoyable reminder of a historic performance by Danny Kerry's side. Captain Kate Richardson-Walsh and her colleagues won eight games from eight, culminating in a penalty-shoot-out victory over the Netherlands, the two-time reigning champions, to clinch gold medals and a central role in the post-Games narrative.

Following in the footsteps of Richard Dodds' 1988 men's team, the likes of Maddie Hinch, five-goal Alex Danson and Crista Cullen have joined Richardson-Walsh and wife Helen, who scored four times as well as converting in the decisive shoot-out, in inspiring the next generation. "Do you remember 1988?" Kate Richardson-Walsh asked afterwards. "I was eight, I know it increased interest in hockey." The hope will now be that a new generation are inspired to take up the game and follow in the footsteps of the 2016 champions.

A younger generation has already made their presence felt within the squad. After a bronze medal at London 2012, a number of youthful players have come into and strengthened the team. Lily Owsley scored four goals and Nicola White three in the tournament – Owsley opening the scoring in the final before White forced penalties – while Sophie

Bray struck twice and caught the eye with her superb ball skills. Australia and the United States were among the scalps taken in Pool B – those two, along with Argentina, joined Team GB in the quarter-finals – while the Netherlands topped Pool A after four wins and a draw with New Zealand. Team GB saw off Spain 3-1 in the quarter-final and a Danson double helped them sweep aside New Zealand 3-0 in the semis to set up a showdown with the world's top side, who beat Argentina 3-2 and needed penalties to get past Germany.

Owsley's goal was cancelled out by Kitty van Male and the Dutch twice took the lead, through Maartje

Paumen and Van Male again, only for first Cullen and then White to hit back. Goalkeeper Hinch then took centre stage, her meticulous preparation and unorthodox angles of attack proving too much for the Dutch, while Helen Richardson-Walsh scored after Georgie Twigg was fouled by Dutch keeper Joyce Sombroek and Hollie Webb netted the clinching goal.

While the men's team were unable to progress from their group in a tournament won by Argentina, who beat Belgium 4-2 in the final, the women ensured the tournament and its result will live long in the memory – at least as long as "1988 and all that".

"The London cycle turned everything around. We started to get loads of belief. It shows that if you dedicate your life to something you can make it happen."

Helen Richardson-Walsh.

Left: Team GB's Adam Dixon (left) celebrates his goal against Brazil with Iain Lewers.

Above: Goalkeeper Maddie Hinch saves a penalty from Netherlands' Maartje Paumen.

Below: Team GB players on the podium to collect their historic gold medals.

Right: Gauthier Boccard's brilliant goal for Belgium was in vain in the men's final.

Webb holds nerve

The hopes of the nation rested on Hollie Webb's shoulders and she held her nerve to convert her penalty in the shoot-out against the Netherlands to spark wild celebrations. "I tried to block everything out and think 'this is just at Bisham (Abbey), I'm just practising'," she said. "I'd done my homework, I knew going up what I was going to do. I didn't actually feel nervous."

Boccard beauty

It may not have been much consolation for Gauthier Boccard after he finished on the losing team but the Belgian scored one of the goals of the tournament in their defeat to Argentina in the final. Boccard beat three men before smashing a fierce shot into the corner to set up a thrilling finale but it was not enough as a late goal clinched a 4-2 victory for the South Americans.

Judo

The judo was held in the Carioca Arena 2, which is to become a permanent training centre for a variety of sports. Judo has featured at the Olympic Games since Tokyo 1964, with women's events added at Barcelona 1992.

Events

Men's -60kg
Men's -66kg
Men's -73kg
Men's -81kg
Men's -90kg
Men's -100kg
Men's +100kg
Women's -48kg
Women's -52kg
Women's -57kg
Women's -63kg
Women's -70kg
Women's -78kg
Women's +78kg

Team GB's Sally Conway (right) in action against Colombia's Yuri Alvear in the women's -70kg semi-final.

Judo

Team GB's judokas performed to their potential in competitive fields, securing one medal and exciting with their aggression throughout their time in Rio.

In the training camps leading up to the Olympic Games it was hoped that Team GB's judo athletes would be able to come away with a medal. When they finally arrived in Rio, it was Sally Conway who capped a promising team performance by taking a bronze medal home.

It was perhaps appropriate that Britain's medal came in the -70kg division, given elite performance coach Kate Howey MBE won silver there at Sydney 2000. Conway first fought Tunisia's Houda Miled and was superbly awarded the ippon in under a minute when forcing her opponent to tap out. France's Gevrise Emane was next and in a tight, tense match-up, she impressed again in coming from behind to secure the ippon.

In her quarter-final, against Israel's Linda Bolder, she built on an early shido against her opponent with a waza-ari and then the ippon that secured her progress to the final four. Colombia's Yuri Alvear, a three-time world champion, was Conway's opponent. In her most competitive match yet, golden score was necessary to separate them and was concluded when Alvear eventually secured a waza-ari to reach the final.

Conway finally faced Austria's Bernadette Graf in the bronze-medal match and, after falling behind early on, swiftly recovered to build a lead she would not give up, taking

bronze – the least she deserved for an impressive performance. Japan's Haruka Tachimoto won gold.

Conway said: "It's amazing. I'm so happy. I can't even put it into words. One minute you've got a chance of becoming an Olympic champion, the next you're fighting for a bronze medal. It was such a quick turnover. I didn't have time to think. I just had to get that bronze after everything I've put myself through here."

Ashley McKenzie was Britain's competitor in the men's -60kg category and in his opening match he defeated Turkey's Bekir Ozlu with three yuko scores after a confident display. His challenge was ended in the last 16 by Kazakhstan's Yeldos Smetov in a highly competitive

contest which Smetov won by a single yuko.

In the -66kg, the more tactical Colin Oates was drawn with France's Kilian Le Blouch. An even affair went to golden score and concluded in victory for Le Blouch when Oates was deemed to have committed a false attack and picked up a shido. Nekoda Smythe-Davis competed in the -57kg category and defeated Austria's Sabrina Filzmoser to progress to the next stage against France's Automne Pavia. From there, the experienced Pavia retained the edge over Smythe-Davis's aggression, earning a yuko when both were on a shido.

In the -63kg, Alice Schlesinger drew South Korea's Ji-Yun Bak and won a tight contest with an ippon after a lovely throw. The Netherlands' Anicka van Emden was her opponent in the next stage but, after an aggressive start, Schlesinger was eliminated by a single shido.

In the men's -100kg, Ben Fletcher was unfortunate to meet Georgia's Beka Gviniashvili, and after falling behind, lost following an ippon. Natalie Powell went straight into the round of 16 of the women's -78kg and defeated Gabon's Sarah Myriam Mazouz via ippon to reach the quarters. There she met France's Andrey Tcheumeo but lost a competitive match after conceding two penalties.

"I didn't get much sleep so I didn't really have anything to wake up for, I've just been thinking about it all night, I can't stop smiling, I'm so happy. "

Sally Conway on her bronze medal.

Sally can wait

Sally Conway held her nerve to become one of Team GB's most unlikely medallists in Rio. The 29-year-old had never won a medal at world or European level before but chose the perfect time to make her big breakthrough with victory in a tense bronze-medal contest. "London 2012 was such an amazing experience for me, but also such a massive disappointment," said Conway afterwards. "So four years later, to come away with a bronze medal at Rio 2016 is all worth it."

Power to the Popole

Refugee athlete Popole Misenga vowed to one day win an Olympic medal after making his Games debut in Rio. The 24-year-old, part of the first Refugee Olympic Team, fled the war-torn Democratic Republic of Congo as a child and has not seen his family for 15 years. He sought asylum in Brazil after the world championships were held in Rio in 2013. Misenga won his opening contest in the -90kg division but was then beaten by top-seeded South Korean Gwak Dong-han in the second round.

Above: Sally Conway (in blue) gets the better of Austria's Bernadette Graf in the bronze-medal match.

Left: Conway's delight is clear as she mounts the medal podium.

Opposite page: Nekoda Smythe-Davis after her win over Austria's Sabrina Filzmoser.

Below: Popole Misenga made his mark as he competed under the banner of the Refugee Olympic Team.

Modern Pentathlon

The modern pentathlon was staged at three venues, the Deodoro Aquatics Centre, Deodoro Stadium and Youth Arena. All five disciplines – fencing, swimming, horse riding, shooting and running – took place across two days.

Events

Men's individual
Women's individual

Team GB's Joe Choong in action in the final discipline of the modern pentathlon, the combined run and shoot.

Modern Pentathlon

Despite encouraging performances and Olympic records, Team GB were unable to repeat Samantha Murray's medal-winning performance at London 2012 in the modern pentathlon.

The challenge of the modern pentathlon is to make sure you are consistently good across all phases and, after the swimming, fencing and showjumping events, Joe Choong was just that and in the mix to become Team GB's first male medallist in the individual event. Given the sport has been omnipresent since Stockholm 1912, it would have been some achievement for a 21-year-old Londoner to claim a top-three spot.

Ahead of the final combined running and shooting event, Choong was in second spot but misses in the second and third shooting efforts dropped him out of medal contention. Even so, a 10th-placed finish was better than the youngster could have hoped for before boarding the plane to Brazil and his

sights are already set on Tokyo 2020 in four years' time, where he knows he can shoot better.

"I know that coming into the competition I wouldn't have been disappointed coming 10th," he said. "I showed in my first shoot, when I got five out of five, what I could do, then I couldn't hit the target. I knew if I had shot like I normally do, I would have got a medal, so that gives me great confidence moving forward but I am not going to make excuses."

He also managed to finish four places ahead of University of Bath teammate Jamie Cooke, who had entered the competition as the world number one. His score in the fencing essentially ruled him out of medal contention but he was at least able to leave Rio having broken a modern pentathlon Olympic record in the

200 metres freestyle swimming by clocking a time of 1:55:60.

The women were aiming to win a medal in the individual event for the fifth Games since the sport's introduction in 2000, when Steph Cook won the first gold and Kate Allenby was third. As then, two women harboured aspirations of reaching the podium, Samantha Murray – second at London 2012 four years earlier – and Kate French. Murray's highlights were a fourth-placed finish in the swimming and eight successive victories in the bonus fencing round while French finished joint top in the showjumping round. French would claim sixth place, a big upgrade after being down in 19th spot after the fencing, while Murray, who has hinted she may not continue to Tokyo in four years' time, was ninth.

"He has come here to his first Games, probably one of the youngest competitors here, and when he goes away and thinks about it, he should be so proud. He has a massive future."

Jamie Cooke on teammate Joe Choong.

Agony for Choong

Although Team GB have never won a men's individual modern pentathlon medal in the Olympic Games, Joe Choong came close to ending that statistic. In second place going into the final combined running and shooting discipline, the 21-year-old was left to rue a disappointing shooting phase which ended any hopes of a medal.

Lesun shines

Russia's Aleksander Lesun and Australia's Chloe Esposito both broke the Olympic points record to win gold in the modern pentathlon. Lesun was in contention for glory at London 2012 only to wilt in the shooting discipline, yet this time he kept his cool to finish ahead of Ukraine's Pavlo Tymoshchenko and Mexico's Ismael Hernandez Uscanga. Esposito did it differently, surging through in the combined run-and-shooting stage having been out of the medals until the final stage.

Top: Samantha Murray takes on Canada's Melanie McCann in the fencing.

Left: Kate French competes in the swimming section of the women's modern pentathlon.

Opposite page: Team GB's Joe Choong (second left) and Jamie Cooke (right) compete in the modern pentathlon at the Deodoro Stadium.

Rowing

The Lagoa Rodrigo de Freitas hosted the rowing regatta under the watchful eye of Christ the Redeemer. Eight men's and six women's events took place across six days.

Events

Men's & Women's single sculls
Men's & Women's double sculls
Men's & Women's quadruple sculls
Men's & Women's coxless pair
Men's & Women's coxed eight
Men's & Women's lightweight double sculls
Men's coxless four
Men's lightweight coxless four

Katherine Grainger and Vicky Thornley start off in their quest for a medal underneath Sugarloaf Mountain.

Rowing

3 **2**

Team GB battled tricky conditions to produce a rowing display packed with history, medals and memorable moments, ultimately remaining the sport's top Olympic nation.

Expectation was great on Team GB's rowers going into Rio 2016 and once again they delivered. Thanks to a successful three-day spell that yielded a trio of golds and a pair of silvers, Great Britain proved their world-class credentials on the water to top the medal table for the third successive Games.

It started with second place for history-maker Katherine Grainger and her partner Vicky Thornley in the double sculls before the gold rush began when Helen Glover and Heather Stanning's triumph in the women's pair was quickly followed by victory for the men's four. A 'Super Saturday' wrapped up the regatta in style as the men's eight grabbed gold after the corresponding women's crew secured silver – their first Olympic medal. The successes put Britain two medals clear of any other nation, once more displaying Team GB's dominance in the sport.

Elsewhere on the Lagoa, Alan Campbell's hopes in the single sculls were ruined by illness while the men's quad sculls eventually finished fifth after they suffered a setback when Graeme Thomas's virus led to a change in the boat within hours of him landing in South America. Alan Sinclair and Stewart Innes fell agonisingly outside the medal places in the men's pairs and there was also frustration for Jonathan Walton and John Collins, who were fifth in the double sculls.

The overriding emotion at the end was far from disappointment, though. Golden pair Glover and Stanning more than lived up to their tag as favourites as they stormed to victory to become the first female British rowers to retain their Olympic crown. Four years on from lighting up London 2012, their unbeaten run, which stretches back to 2011, was never in doubt on a dank, dismal day in Brazil.

They led from the outset, powering their way to a commanding position before holding off a late surge from New Zealanders Genevieve Behrent and Rebecca Scown to secure a winning margin of 1.24 seconds. It was phenomenal stuff from a remarkable duo and they embraced exhausted at the finish line in the knowledge they had justified the pre-race hype. The world and European champions were 1.77 seconds up after 500 metres and 3.58 seconds ahead at the halfway mark. The New Zealand boat pushed hard to make up the gap but was forced to settle for silver, with Danish pair Hedvig Rasmussen and Anne Andersen, who had come so close to beating Glover and Stanning in the heats, taking bronze.

> ## "This is not being good once, it's being good every day, every race. It just feels so good with all the pressure we put on ourselves."

Helen Glover after retaining the women's pair title with Heather Stanning.

Above: Helen Glover and Heather Stanning clinch gold in the women's pair.

Opposite page: Glover (right) and Stanning celebrate back on dry land.

Top right: Alan Sinclair and Stewart Innes just missed out on a medal in the men's equivalent.

Bottom right: Katherine Grainger and Vicky Thornley collected silver in the double sculls event.

Glover felt the success topped the achievement of picking up her first gold medal on home soil four years earlier. "I think it means so much more," the 30-year-old said. "We put an awful lot of pressure on ourselves. I've been so emotional this week and this is not me at all. I know it was a home Games and there's nothing more special, but this was defending a title. This is not being good once, it's being good every day, every race. It just feels so good with all the pressure we put on ourselves."

It was Team GB's first rowing gold of the Games and they did not have to wait long for another. The second came within 20 minutes, courtesy of Alex Gregory, Constantine Louloudis, George Nash and Mohamed Sbihi.

They went into the men's four as favourites on the back of World Cup wins in Poznan and Lucerne and lived up to their billing with a comfortable winning margin over silver medallists Australia and the third-placed Italians. "Crossing the line, relief is the overwhelming emotion," said Gregory, the only remaining member of the victorious London 2012 boat. "Relief that this day is over, this week is over, this year is over. Relief that it all paid off. We got that race. It was our perfect race. I wouldn't change a stroke in that race. This last week, I haven't enjoyed it. It was not fun because of the tension and nerves. This feeling now makes it worth it."

The victory maintained Britain's stranglehold on the event which dates back to Sydney 2000 and the final Games of Sir Steve Redgrave and was yet another success for Britain's most prolific Olympic coach Jurgen Grobler. After winning titles at an extraordinary 10 Games in a row, the 70-year-old German admits retirement may be on the cards before Tokyo 2020 comes around because he 'doesn't like to limp'.

There were no signs of anyone limping in Rio, though, and it was

"We got that race. It was our perfect race. I wouldn't change a stroke in that race."

Alex Gregory on Team GB's gold medal-winning performance in the men's four.

Left: Constantine Louloudis, George Nash, Mohamed Sbihi and Alex Gregory on their way to gold in the men's four.

Below left: Team GB's women's eight celebrate an historic silver medal.

a familiar face who kicked off the medal haul as Grainger recorded her 'greatest achievement' to become the most-decorated female British Olympian. Success for the 40-year-old Scot and her 28-year-old Welsh teammate Thornley came after she revealed the high winds and choppy waters on the Lagoa were the worst Olympic conditions she had faced. The elements were so severe they led to the boat of Serbs Milos Vasic and Nenad Bedik capsizing and many rowers voicing frustrations before the second day of action had to be postponed. Nevertheless, Grainger's hard work and dedication paid off when it mattered, although she narrowly missed out on retaining the gold won with Anna Watkins in 2012 by the smallest of margins. Polish pair Magdalena Fularczyk-Kozlowska and Natalia Madaj pipped the British duo to first place, overtaking them in the latter stages to finish 0.95 seconds ahead, while Lithuania took third.

Grainger, who first competed at the Olympics in 2000, now has a gold and four silvers from five successive Games, putting her level with tennis player Kitty Godfree – but with a

stronger collection of medals – and one ahead of four-time swimming medallist Rebecca Adlington and four-time cycling gold medallist Laura Trott. The latest comes less than two years after returning to the sport having completed a PhD in the sentencing of homicide at King's College London. Her achievement was even more impressive given that she was more than a decade older than all of the other medallists in her discipline and 18 years senior to bronze-winning Lithuanian Milda Valciukaite.

"Considering what we've been through the last couple of years, I'm so proud of what we've done," Grainger said. "It's a medal that not many would have put money on. I thought if I could come out with a medal of any kind here it would be my greatest achievement. There were many, many dark days. So to stand here with a medal around our necks makes it all worthwhile."

Like Glover and Stanning, the men's eight led throughout their final race. They finished well clear of the German and Dutch boats to reclaim the title for Britain for the first time in 16 years.

Crew members Andrew Triggs Hodge and Pete Reed are now three-time Olympic gold medallists, having won in the men's four in Beijing and London, with Scott Durant, Tom Ransley, Matt Gotrel, Paul Bennett, Matt Langridge, Will Satch and cox Phelan Hill completing the victorious line-up.

History had earlier been made by the women's eight of Katie Greves, Melanie Wilson, Frances Houghton, Polly Swann, Jessica Eddie, Olivia Carnegie-Brown, Karen Bennett, Zoe Lee and cox Zoe De Toledo. They became the first female British eight crew to take a podium place at the Olympics after snatching silver from Romania, with the USA a couple of seconds out of reach.

An emotional Houghton said: "Sport can be so much pressure but at the same time sport is supposed to be fun and a great experience. It's something you do that you enjoy and you pursue because you like to be challenged.

"It's not only about us nine girls. There was a group of 14 who came into the team at the beginning of the year. For every single one of those girls we were carrying that."

Left: The men's coxed eight crew celebrate winning Team GB's third gold medal of the rowing regatta.

Below: Men's eight crew member Will Satch kisses his girlfriend as the celebrations begin in earnest.

Below left: The scene in Rio during the women's eight final, won by USA (right).

Bottom: Mahe Drysdale (top) pips Croatian rower Damir Martin after a photo-finish.

For the record

Olympic Records
Rowing – Men's single sculls
Mahe Drysdale (New Zealand) 6.41:34sec

Great eight

Britain's women had never before won a medal in the coxed eight in the 40 years rowing had been open to them as an Olympic event. All that changed on the final day of the rowing regatta in Rio, though, as the team sneaked silver ahead of Romania in the closing stages of the race to write their names into the country's record books.

The tightest of margins

Was there a more unlucky athlete in Rio than Damir Martin? The Croat's 6.41.34sec in the men's single sculls was a dead heat for first place with Mahe Drysdale according to the official clock. After studying a photo finish, officials declared Drysdale the winner by one 5,000th of a second as the New Zealander retained his title and recorded an Olympic record to leave Martin bemoaning his misfortune.

Rugby Sevens

The 15-man code had featured between 1900 and 1924 but the faster, shorter format of rugby sevens made its debut at the Rio 2016 Olympic Games.

Events

Men's tournament
Women's tournament

Team GB's Mark Bennett is tackled by Vatemo Ravouvou of Fiji in the final of the men's rugby sevens.

Rugby Sevens

Rugby sevens made a scintillating Olympic Games debut and Team GB more than played its part. The standard proved world class, making a silver medal in the men's competition even more of an achievement.

Team GB were the only nation to play off for a medal in both the men's and women's rugby sevens tournaments as the sport made its Olympic debut in Rio. Led by captain Tom Mitchell, the men's team claimed silver as Fiji secured their first-ever Olympic medal with a 43-7 win in the final.

One of the iconic moments of the Olympic Games was Mitchell and his team mixing with Fiji, and bronze medallists South Africa, on the podium after receiving their medals to mark the Pacific nation's historic success. It was a heart-warming show of sportsmanship as Team GB put the disappointment of their final defeat to one side and posed for the cameras shoulder to shoulder with their conquerors, who became instant heroes in their homeland.

It was a poignant end to a memorable six days of rugby at the Deodoro Stadium, during which both Team GB teams took centre stage following unbeaten group-stage campaigns. Captain Emily Scarratt's women's team conceded only three points in the opening round as they cast aside Brazil, Japan and Canada, who would ultimately beat them 33-10 in the bronze-medal match.

Team GB ran in 15 tries during the group phase, with the threat so evenly spread that no-one crossed for more than two scores. Abbie Brown then opened her own account with a double in the 26-7 quarter-final win over Fiji – her first coming after only 17 seconds – but yellow cards proved their undoing in the medal rounds as they were beaten by New Zealand and then Canada.

The men's team also coasted through their group as they overcame New Zealand, Japan and Kenya by piling on the second most points of any team. The free-scoring did not translate to the knockout phase, however, as Team GB needed nerves of steel to progress to the final.

Dan Bibby was the hero of a tense quarter-final when he crashed over for the game's only try in extra time. Argentina had missed a penalty to win the game, and the drama continued when Mitchell saw a kick rebound off the post in extra time before Bibby dived over.

A 7-5 semi-final win over South Africa was just as gripping, as Dan Norton's try was converted by Mitchell after Team GB had trailed at half-time. That set up the emotional final where Fiji's desire for a historic gold proved insurmountable.

"I had a few tears at the end. Everyone has worked so hard, and it has been an amazing journey. It is a nice little way to finish it with a silver medal. "

Team GB men's captain **Tom Mitchell**.

Nifty Norton

The men's semi-final against South Africa proved a low-scoring affair and Team GB were trailing 5-0 at half-time after conceding inside the first two minutes. The decisive moment was provided when Dan Norton once again illustrated his blistering pace, bursting through the line and touching down under the posts to give Tom Mitchell a simple conversion which ultimately proved enough to secure a place in the final.

Fiji make history

Fiji had not won a single medal since their debut at a summer Olympic Games 60 years ago, and the emotion of their 43-7 success in the men's final against Team GB was visible when the hulking presences that had bash, crashed and offloaded their way to a seven-try victory were left stunned into silence by an achievement that made them instant heroes in their homeland.

Top: Players from all three medal teams, Fiji, Team GB and South Africa, mingle on the podium.

Above left: Abbie Brown crosses for one of her two tries in the Team GB women's quarter-final win over Fiji.

Left: Fiji fans celebrate the first Olympic medal ever won by the Pacific islanders.

Opposite page: Team GB skipper Tom Mitchell gets a kiss from teammate Dan Bibby as they show off their medals.

Sailing

Sailing first featured at the Olympic Games in 1900. In 2016 the waters of Guanabara Bay saw 11 days of action across five men's, four women's and one mixed event.

Events

Men's & Women's RS:X
Men's & Women's 470
Men's Laser
Men's Finn
Men's 49er
Women's Laser Radial
Women's 49er FX
Nacra 17

Giles Scott continued Team GB's remarkable domination of the Finn class.

Sailing

Team GB enjoyed a successful Games on Guanabara Bay, winning three medals — two gold — and topping sailing's medal table, while Nick Dempsey became the most decorated Olympic windsurfer of all time.

Sailing

Team GB returned to the top of the medal table as Giles Scott continued the country's 16-year dominance in the Finn class before Saskia Clark and Hannah Mills ended their 470 partnership in style. Scott followed in Sir Ben Ainslie's wake to win the Finn, the nation's fifth successive gold medal in the event, while Clark sailed off into the sunset by claiming 470 gold with Mills.

There were near misses for further medals. London 2012 silver medallist Luke Patience and his partner Chris Grube came fifth in the men's 470, an outstanding achievement given they paired up only eight months earlier after Patience's previous teammate Elliot Willis was diagnosed with bowel cancer. Meanwhile, in the Laser class two-time world champion Nick Thompson was sixth and women's world champion Alison Young eighth only eight weeks after breaking an ankle.

But the two golds were enough to return the team to the top of the sailing medal table. "It is fantastic to top the medal podium," said Royal Yachting Association Olympic manager Stephen Park. "We were knocked off the top of the medal table four years ago by Australia. We had been top of the medal table in Sydney, Athens and Beijing, so it's nice to be back on the top."

The pressure was on Scott in the Finn. Ainslie had won in Athens, Beijing and London while Iain Percy had started the golden run at Sydney 2000. Scott, who missed out on a berth in the Finn to Ainslie four years ago, dominated the event in Rio, securing the gold medal with a race to spare.

"There's not many times you can say you have won an Olympic Games before the medal race."

Giles Scott.

"There's not many times you can say you have won an Olympic Games before the medal race," Scott said. "It started with Percy in Sydney and then went on with Ben from 2004 to 2012. (Coach) Matt (Howard) and I have really just evolved what has gone before us."

Mills and Clark also highlighted their superiority in the 470 by securing an upgrade on their London 2012 silver ahead of the medal race. After a delay of 24 hours due to a lack of wind, the pair eased home in eighth before starting their celebrations and, in Clark's case, retirement. "That's it for me," she said. "If I think about it, that this is the end, I might start crying. It's been amazing, winning a gold medal with one of your best mates."

Windsurfing

The 36-year-old Nick Dempsey was the most experienced member of Team GB's sailing team and he secured his medal

Golden Grael

There were wild celebrations after Kahene Kunza and Martine Grael – daughter of sailing great Torben – triumphed in the 49erFX. The final action of the Olympic sailing regatta ended in glory for the hosts as the Brazilian duo won the medal race to become champions. The boat was carried to shore on the shoulders of excitable locals, with Grael following in the footsteps of her five-time Olympic medallist father Torben.

Double Dutch

Dorian van Rijsselberghe was so dominant in the men's event that he only had to show up for the medal race to secure his second successive Olympic title. That would not have been in keeping with the Dutchman's ability though and he instead ensured a suitable climax by winning the medal race, which became a victory procession as he repeated his London 2012 success.

when he finished fourth in the medal race to claim silver and match his achievement from London 2012 in finishing runner-up to Dorian van Rijsselberghe of the Netherlands.

Dempsey was beaming after adding silver to his bronze from Athens 2004 and the second place at London 2012, which saw him enter the record books as the most decorated men's Olympic windsurfer. "It is amazing," he said. "It is awesome, something I am incredibly proud of. It has been a long time, I have been working for a long time and it is very hard to stay at the top for that long."

Dempsey has hinted he might bow out at the top but suggested there was a slight chance he could continue on to Tokyo 2020. "I am not sure I can do it again," he said. "I would love to if I could."

In the women's event, Bryony Shaw ended her regatta in ninth place and is now focused on coming back stronger in Tokyo in four years' time. "I feel like I have had bad fortune but it has been a great four years," said Shaw, who won bronze at the Beijing Games in 2008.

Top: Saskia Clark and Hannah Mills in action in the 470 class medal race, by which time they had already secured gold, emulating Scott's achievement.

Opposite: Giles Scott celebrates winning gold in the Finn, making it five successive Games at which Team GB has won the class following the exploits of Iain Percy and three-time winner Sir Ben Ainslie.

Above: Dempsey with his second successive silver medal.

Right: Beijing medallist Bryony Shaw had to settle for ninth place.

Shooting

The firing range for the shooting was at the Olympic Shooting Centre in Deodoro. The seven shooting ranges used for the 2007 Pan American Games underwent some minor improvements while a temporary range was also built.

Events

Men's & Women's 10m air pistol
Men's & Women's 10m air rifle
Men's 25m rapid fire pistol
Men's 50m pistol
Women's 25m pistol
Men's 50m rifle prone
Men's & Women's 50m rifle three positions
Men's & Women's skeet
Men's & Women's trap
Men's double trap

Somerset farmer Ed Ling celebrates taking the bronze medal after a shoot-out in the men's trap competition.

Shooting

Team GB's talented shooting team brought home two medals from Rio 2016, an increase on the single gold achieved at London 2012, and all indications are even more is to come at Tokyo 2020.

Team GB was represented in Rio by a shooting team labelled beforehand by leader Phil Scanlan as "the most talented we've taken abroad to an Olympic Games in terms of depth". And while none of the six-strong group were quite able to emulate the achievement of Peter Wilson, who won the nation's first Olympic shooting medal for 12 years at London 2012 with gold in the double trap, there was still plenty to celebrate.

It was third time lucky for Ed Ling as the 33-year-old Somerset farmer, 25th on his Olympic debut in Athens and then 21st in London, claimed trap bronze on the first Monday in Brazil. Having come joint-fourth out of six in the first phase of the final, Ling secured his spot in the bronze-medal contest by winning a shoot-off against Egypt's Ahmed Kamar. The 2014 world silver medallist then beat Czech David Kostelecky 13-9 in the third-place decider to seal bronze, before admitting he would soon be back to baling straw on his return to his family's Taunton farm.

Two days on from that, there was another bronze for Team GB as Steven Scott emerged triumphant from a showdown with his teammate Tim Kneale in the double trap event. Scott and Kneale faced off for the medal after being in a three-way tie for third and subsequently ousting Australian James Willett in a shoot-off.

Scott then added to his 2014 Commonwealth gold as he produced a maximum score to see off world record-holder and 2015 world silver medallist Kneale 30-28. Thirty-one-year-old Lewisham-born Scott, who had been working with Wilson's Dubai-based coach Sheikh Ahmed Al Maktoum in preparation for the Games, said of beating his compatriot Kneale: "It is very emotional. There is a little part of me that wanted him to win as well."

History was made in that event as Kuwaiti Fehaid Aldeehani became the first competitor under the International Olympic Committee flag to capture gold. And there was more towards the end of the week when American Kim Rhode won bronze in the women's skeet to become the first Olympian to claim medals at six consecutive summer Games.

That event featured British teenager Amber Hill, on whom there had been considerable attention in the build-up to the Games. The 2015 European Games gold medallist from Berkshire, who uses bespoke pink cartridges on the firing range, qualified for the first phase of the final on what was her Olympic debut, ending up sixth.

"I was a bit cheeky after London. I said 'Pete, if you are thinking about retiring, pretty please ask Sheikh Ahmed Al Maktoum if he will work with me.' He is a phenomenal coach – the best in the world."

Steven Scott on working with coach Sheikh Ahmed Al Maktoum after Peter Wilson's retirement.

Above: Steven Scott (left) and Team GB colleague Tim Kneale after their shoot-out for bronze in the men's double trap.

Left: Scott shows off his bronze medal after pipping his teammate 30-28.

Right: Teenager Amber Hill celebrates reaching the final of the women's skeet in her first Olympic Games.

Below right: Kuwaiti shooter Fehaid Aldeehani made history by winning gold while competing under the IOC flag.

Battle of Britons

Team GB team-mates Steven Scott and Tim Kneale found themselves in the awkward position of competing against each other in the battle for the bronze medal in a shootout in the men's double trap competition. Scott was immaculate in wet and blustery conditions to claim the last place on the podium with a perfect score but the embrace at the end proved there were no hard feelings between the pair and Scott admitted afterwards: "It is very emotional."

IOC champion

Kuwait-born Fehaid Aldeehani made history with his men's double trap triumph, becoming the first competitor under the International Olympic Committee flag to win gold. Kuwait are banned from taking part in the Games due to government interference in the country's Olympic movement. The Olympic flag was raised at the medal ceremony for Aldeehani, who has won two bronze medals at previous Games, with the Olympic anthem also played.

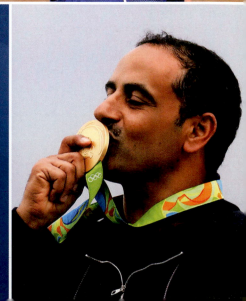

Table Tennis

One of the most popular racket sports in the world, table tennis has featured at the Olympic Games since Seoul 1988 and in Rio was staged at Riocentro Pavilion 3, which featured four official competition tables.

Events

Men's singles
Men's team
Women's singles
Women's team

Paul Drinkhall was one of two Team GB table tennis players to qualify for the Games through their world ranking, and made a fine run to the last 16 of the men's singles.

Table Tennis

For the first time in two decades, two British men, Liam Pitchford and Paul Drinkhall, qualified for the Games through their world rankings, with Drinkhall making the fourth round at Rio 2016.

Team GB took a three-strong team of Liam Pitchford, Paul Drinkhall and Sam Walker to Rio, with Pitchford and Drinkhall also entering the men's singles competition. Their Games may have concluded without a medal but their performance was considered their best at an Olympic Games.

There is also significant optimism surrounding their future. The trio reached the quarter-finals but were only eliminated after testing China, who featured three of the world's top four players and won gold in the men's and women's singles and both team events. All three matches of the 3-0 defeat went to four games and Pitchford and Drinkhall both led their singles matches 1-0, the former

against world number one Ma Long. Drinkhall then combined with Walker in the doubles, against Xu and 2012 singles champion Zhang Jike. Beyond a dominant opening game for China, Team GB were very competitive.

They had overcome France in the opening round to ensure their progress, doing so dramatically. Walker, on his Olympic debut, had won five consecutive points from 10-7 down, having saved three match points, to defeat Simon Gauzy when France were on the verge of the quarter-finals to ensure a 3-2 win for Team GB. Gauzy had earlier beaten Pitchford and while Drinkhall won against Emmanuel Lebesson, he also combined with Walker in a doubles loss to Lebesson and Tristan

Flore that left them 2-1 down and needing to win the last two matches to reach the quarters. Pitchford levelled by overcoming Flore, setting the stage for Walker's entertaining victory.

Drinkhall's run to the last 16 of the singles competition was ended by a 4-2 defeat to Vladimir Samsonov of Belarus. He had already secured wins over two higher-ranked opponents to become only the third Briton to reach the last 16 at a Games, following Carl Prean in 1992 and Desmond Douglas in 1988. In the previous round he defeated Croatia's Andrej Gacina 4-2, having earlier secured a 4-3 second-round win over Singapore's Gao Ning.

Pitchford had won 4-1 against Uzbekistan's Zokhid Kenjaev in the second round, but lost via the same scoreline to Jeoung Youngsik of South Korea in the next. He had been seeded directly into the second round and afterwards his world ranking climbed from 48 to 44. Drinkhall moved up from 58 to 32 while Walker rose from 131 to 117.

"Quarter-finals of the Olympics bodes well for the future so I think we're on the up."

Liam Pitchford on Team GB's progress in table tennis.

Japan test China

China's dominance of the sport continued with victory in the men's final, which completed a clean sweep of all four gold medals. However, they were given a tougher-than-expected test in the final by a young Japan team and, although China ran out 3-1 winners, there was plenty to suggest the silver medallists will be ready to challenge the sport's super power when the Games go to Tokyo in 2020.

Home town hero

Few events produced as much passion from the Brazilian crowd as hometown hero Hugo Calderano's surprise victory in the men's singles against Peng Tang of Hong Kong. About 3,000 fans produced an atmosphere more in keeping with football and roared the world number 54 on, even after he lost the first game. Calderano responded by battling back for victory against an opponent who had been expected to challenge for a medal.

Above: Women's singles gold medallist Ding Ning.

Below: Dramatic multiple exposure shot of British number one Paul Drinkhall.

Opposite left: Men's singles action in the Riocentre Pavilion 3 venue.

Opposite right: Team GB's Liam Pitchford in action.

Taekwondo

There were four weight categories each for men and women as the martial art featured at a fifth successive Olympic Games, having made its debut at Sydney 2000.

Events

Men's -58kg
Men's -68kg
Men's -80kg
Men's +80kg
Women's -49kg
Women's -57kg
Women's -67kg
Women's +67kg

Jade Jones celebrates beating Spain's Eva Calvo Gomez to win gold in the women's 57kg final and retain her Olympic title.

Taekwondo

1 1 1

Team GB sent four fighters to Rio, where Jade Jones looked to defend her title and Lutalo Muhammad aimed to improve on his bronze. Both delivered more success, with Bianca Walkden also returning with a medal.

Four years ago in London, Jade Jones came into the Olympic Games as a teenager determined to prove herself against the best. At Rio 2016, the 'Headhunter' was now very much the target for those determined to take her under-57kg crown. But any questions over whether the Flint fighter had the required mentality to deliver a second Olympic title at the age of only 23 were once again answered in emphatic fashion. Jones produced all the way through the competition, which culminated in a stunning 16-7 victory over Eva Calvo Gomez of Spain, her long-time rival, in the gold-medal contest.

For Lutalo Muhammad, however, there was to be heartbreak. Having defeated double Olympic champion Steven Lopez in the quarter-finals, hopes of another gold for Team GB in the men's under-80kg division were dashed in the very last second as Cheick Sallah Cisse landed a crucial head kick to secure a dramatic 8-6 victory – and with it a first Olympic title for the Ivory Coast. Muhammad was distraught in an emotional post-fight interview, the 25-year-old from Walthamstow battling back the tears. "I am proud I contributed to GB's record-breaking medal tally but it should have been a gold," Muhammad said. "But I am absolutely gutted to blow it like that. I will have to wait four years for another chance."

Bianca Walkden was another member of Team GB who had come to Rio with their sights firmly set on gold. The 24-year-old 2015 World Championship heavyweight champion was soon making an impact. Walkden confidently progressed to the women's over-67kg semi-final against Zheng Shuyin of China for a shot at the gold-medal fight. However, it was another moment of bitter disappointment as Shuyin, who would go on to become Olympic champion, landed a winning head kick in golden score to leave Walkden facing a repechage fight for bronze. The Liverpudlian, though, regrouped to return to Carioca Arena 3 a few hours later with complete focus as she saw off Moroccan Wiam Dislam 7-1 to claim a place on the podium in her first Olympic Games.

Team GB's fighters almost delivered a clean sweep of medals but Mahama Cho came up just short in his bronze match. Cho, the 27-year-old, born in the Ivory Coast and who moved to London aged eight, was unable to recover after his 4-1 semi-final defeat against Radik Isaev of Azerbaijan, the eventual champion. Brazilian Maicon de Andrade Siqueira delighted the home crowd as he beat Cho 5-4 to win bronze.

"There's no reason why she can't do the treble if she wants but it is a hard commitment over four years."

GB Taekwondo coach **Paul Green** on double gold medallist Jade Jones.

Opposite left: Jade Jones celebrates a second successive Olympic gold medal.

Below: Lutalo Muhammad is left distraught after falling a mere one second short of winning Olympic gold.

Above left: Bianca Walkden won bronze in the women's heavyweight division.

Above: Team GB's Mahama Cho in action.

Lutalo is so close

Welsh fighter Jade Jones became a double Olympic champion in the women's under-57kg category, but the most dramatic moment came when Lutalo Muhammad was just one second away from winning gold in the men's under-80kg division when he conceded a kick, resulting in a silver medal instead.

Thirst for firsts

Cheick Sallah Cisse, claiming a first Olympic gold for Ivory Coast was not the only historic moment of the Rio 2016 Taekwondo tournament. Ahmad Abughaush won Jordan's first Olympic medal with under-68kg gold while Kimia Alizadeh Zenoorin became the first female competitor from Iran to win an Olympic medal with bronze at under-57kg.

Tennis

The tennis took place at the purpose-built Olympic Tennis Centre at Barra, which featured 16 courts. The centre court and its facilities are permanent and will be an important sporting legacy from the Games.

Events

Men's singles
Men's doubles
Women's singles
Women's doubles
Mixed doubles

Andy Murray on his way to retaining his Olympic tennis men's singles title by beating Juan Martin Del Potro.

Tennis

Andy Murray headed to Brazil fresh from a second Wimbledon title and looking to successfully defend his Olympic crown. British hopes were high in the women's draw, too, with Johanna Konta making her presence felt.

In 2012 the Olympic tennis tournament helped Andy Murray reach the sport's top table. Four years later it confirmed his place at the head of it. On the grass of Wimbledon in 2012, Murray repaired some of the damage done by his All England Club final defeat to Roger Federer a month earlier. His emphatic victory over the same opponent was the precursor to a maiden grand slam win at the US Open and a first Wimbledon title.

This time, Murray arrived with nothing to prove. A three-time slam winner and recently crowned Wimbledon king again, he was always going to be one of the favourites to take gold once more. Murray's route to the final was a bit of a roller coaster, with the world number two coming close to defeat against both Fabio Fognini and Steve Johnson before finding his form in a semi-final stroll against Kei Nishikori.

Before the Games, it was widely expected his final opponent would be either Novak Djokovic or Rafael Nadal but Juan Martin del Potro thrillingly took care of them both. The popular Argentinian reduced Djokovic to tears with victory in round one and bettered Nadal in a superb semi-final. There was barely a dry eye in the house for Del Potro, who since winning bronze in London had undergone three wrist operations and spent the best part of two years on the sidelines.

Their final was a clash of styles that went on for more than four hours, Del Potro's forehand battering Murray's defences. In the end, Murray found the energy to reach the finish line. His Games started carrying the British flag and ended with tears in his eyes and a second gold around his neck.

Murray became the first player to win two Olympic golds in singles in the process. "I found carrying the flag quite emotional," Murray said of his Games. "I had to regroup and get my mind on the matches so to finish it with a match like that, obviously I was fairly emotional at the end."

Johanna Konta battled through to the quarter-finals, beating two-time grand slam champion Svetlana Kuznetsova, but was undone by Angelique Kerber, who was the final scalp taken by surprise gold medallist Monica Puig. The Murray magic did not transfer to doubles, with Andy hit hard by a first-round loss alongside brother Jamie. The pair had held strong hopes of a medal after their Davis Cup heroics.

There were early losses for Kyle Edmund and Heather Watson in singles along with Watson and Konta and Colin Fleming and Dom Inglot in doubles. Jamie Murray's disappointing Games was completed by a first-round defeat with Konta in mixed doubles. Andy Murray and Watson were late entrants into the field and won their first match but lost their second, with Murray unable to match his London feat of winning two medals. But the 29-year-old's singles exploits cemented his place among tennis' greatest Olympians.

"It was one of the hardest matches I've had to play for a big title."

Andy Murray on retaining his Olympic title.

Andy doubles up

Andy Murray became the first player to win two Olympic golds in singles following a titanic tussle with Juan Martin del Potro. The powerful and popular Argentinian battered the Scot for more than four hours, but Murray's famous defences saw him across the line.

Monica's magic moment

Del Potro provided the fairy tale in the men's singles, but the biggest surprise of the tournament was Monica Puig winning a highly unlikely first gold for Puerto Rico in the women's singles, beating three grand slam winners along the way in Garbine Muguruza, Petra Kvitova in the semi-finals and Angelique Kerber in the gold medal match.

Top: Andy Murray roars with delight at winning gold again.

Opposite page: Murray consoles beaten finalist Juan Martin del Potro.

Above: Monica Puig won Puerto Rico's first Olympic gold.

Left: Johanna Konta in action.

Triathlon

Fort Copacabana provided the start and end points for the triathlon, with the bike stage seeing the competitors head uphill inland before venturing back along the coast for the finish in the 10km run.

Events

Men's individual
Women's individual

Alistair Brownlee crosses the line to win the men's triathlon ahead of brother Jonny.

Triathlon

One of the Games's most memorable images came when brothers Alistair and Jonny Brownlee embraced, having secured a one-two in the men's race while Vicky Holland became Team GB's first female triathlon medallist.

They were seen as Team GB bankers, among the strongest medal hopes the nation had in Brazil, and the Brownlee brothers once again delivered at Copacabana. Yorkshire-based siblings Alistair and Jonny not only repeated their feat four years earlier of both finishing in the top three, they ensured a British one-two finish, Jonny upgrading his bronze to a silver and big brother Alistair becoming the first to retain an Olympic triathlon title.

"When we crossed the line, I can't remember which one of us said it first, but it was very much 'We've done it'. It was fantastic."

Alistair Brownlee.

History was also made in the women's event as Vicky Holland pipped compatriot, teammate and housemate Non Stanford to a bronze in the final metres to gain a first medal for a British female triathlete. The pair train with the Brownlees and it was those painstaking hours in the Yorkshire Dales that ensured Keith and Cathy Brownlee's boys started as the ones to beat in South America. The only man to come between them at London 2012 was Spain's five-time world champion Javier Gomez and he was forced out of Rio a month earlier with a fractured elbow. Alistair had suffered his own injury problems between Olympic Games, undergoing ankle surgery in 2015, but wins in Leeds and Stockholm earlier in the summer showed he was back to peak form.

He and Jonny were in the top six after the 1.5km swim and surged ahead of their rivals up the steep climbs on the bikes, ensuring only France's Vincent Luis was with them by the time they reached the transition to run. Luis dropped off, eventually finishing outside the medals, and Alistair shook off his younger brother on the third lap of four, striding over the line with Yorkshire and British flags before hugging his brother on the floor.

Forty-eight hours later it was the women's turn to try to emulate the Brownlees' achievements and in Holland, Stanford and Helen Jenkins, there was a belief that more medals would be heading back to Britain. All three were in contention for a piece of history after the swim and only Jenkins fell back during the bike phase, though Holland and Stanford were left to settle for a battle for bronze as the United States' Gwen Jorgensen and Olympic champion Nicola Spirig kicked on to claim gold and silver respectively.

As it was, Holland won the last medal by darting ahead with 100 metres to go, leaving her in the unusual position of feeling personal elation at her own achievement and heartbreak for her best friend Stanford at her fourth-placed finish.

Left: The Brownlees celebrate their dream gold-silver.

Above: Athletes emerge from the swim phase in the women's triathlon.

Below: Alistair (left) and Jonny Brownlee clasp hands after collapsing at the finish.

Right: Vicky Holland crosses the line to pip best friend Non Stanford for bronze.

Brotherly love

It was a British one-two in the men's triathlon as Alistair Brownlee led home brother Jonny to become the first in his sport to retain an Olympic title. For Jonny Brownlee, the silver medal represented an upgrade on the bronze medal he won in London. The image of them embracing each other on the ground just past the finish line went viral.

Jorgensen joy

Double world title winner Gwen Jorgensen became an Olympic champion. The 30-year-old was overwhelming favourite having dominated the World Triathlon Series since 2014, though she may not have expected competition from eventual silver medallist Nicola Spirig, who had competed little since taking time off to have a baby after gold in London.

Weightlifting

The weightlifting was staged at Riocentro Pavilion 2, an 11,500-square-metre venue which had been refitted to host the event.

Events

Men's 56kg	Women's 48kg
Men's 62kg	Women's 53kg
Men's 69kg	Women's 58kg
Men's 77kg	Women's 63kg
Men's 85kg	Women's 69kg
Men's 94kg	Women's 75kg
Men's 105kg	Women's +75kg
Men's +105kg	

Rebekah Tiler matched the best lifts of her career as she competed in the women's weightlifting at the age of 17.

Weightlifting

The young athletes representing Team GB were unable to reach the podium but showed exciting promise for the future.

In the women's 69kg B category, the talented 17-year-old Rebekah Tiler impressively equalled two personal bests and a British record to secure a 10th-placed finish with a competitive total of 227kg. The youthful Tiler's first snatch lift, at 98kg, was successful. She missed her second attempt at 101kg but achieved it in her third. The lifter then followed that pattern with a successful clean and jerk attempt at 122kg, missing her second at 126kg, and succeeding with the same weight in her third, to equal her personal best.

Her ultimate total of 227kg equalled her other personal best, and the British record, to take second place in category B. The result concluded a successful period in which Tiler took bronze at April's European Weightlifting Championships and gold at the British National Championships in June. Tiler said: "I just went out and did my best. This was really all about 2020, where I will be aiming for gold." In Rio 2016, though, it was China's Xiang Yanmei who won gold with 261kg. Kazakhstan's Zhazira Zhapparkul secured silver and Egypt's Sara Ahmed took bronze.

In the men's 94kg category, on his Olympic debut and in a sport in which athletes tend to peak at an older age, the 22-year-old Sonny Webster finished 14th of 17. His weight total of 333kg was closer to the 403kg of Iran's eventual gold medallist Sohrab Moradi than the 17th-placed lifter James Adede of Kenya, who stood at 256kg. An 18th lifter did not finish. Webster missed his opening snatch lift at 148kg but responded by succeeding at his second attempt. In his final lift at 151kg, he just fell short. In the clean and jerk, he completed 185kg at the first attempt. He then increased the weight to 190kg, which he was unable to achieve, but succeeded in having secured a competitive total of 333kg.

In doing so, he also took sixth place in the 94kg B category, below that of the Group A which represented the strongest side of the competition. Belarus's Vadzim Straltsou took the silver medal with 395kg, while Lithuania's Aurimas Didzbalis claimed bronze with 392kg.

Below: Team GB's other weightlifter, Sonny Webster, lifted 333kg in the men's 94kg division.

Below right: Rebekah Tiler equalled two personal bests in the women's 69kg category, aged only 17.

"It's amazing to get on the platform and show the rest of the world what I can do. All the crowd were cheering me on no matter who they were supporting."

Rebekah Tiler on her experience at Rio 2016.

Team GB medal count at Rio 2016

	GOLD	SILVER	BRONZE	TOTAL
Athletics	2	1	4	7
Badminton	0	0	1	1
Boxing	1	1	1	3
Canoe Slalom	1	1	0	2
Canoe Sprint	1	1	0	2
Cycling Road	0	0	1	1
Cycling Track	6	4	1	11
Diving	1	1	1	3
Equestrian	2	1	0	3
Golf	1	0	0	1
Gymnastics Artistic	2	1	3	6
Gymnastics Trampoline	0	1	0	1
Hockey	1	0	0	1
Judo	0	0	1	1
Rowing	3	2	0	5
Rugby Sevens	0	1	0	1
Sailing	2	1	0	3
Shooting	0	0	2	2
Swimming	1	5	0	6
Taekwondo	1	1	1	3
Tennis	1	0	0	1
Triathlon	1	1	1	3
TOTAL	27	23	17	67

Team GB Results

'Bring on the Great' was the message that accompanied Team GB and that was what they did as Rio 2016 proved the most successful overseas Games. Every athlete could be proud of their achievement on sport's biggest stage and this section lists all the members of Team GB and their performances.

AQUATICS

DIVING

Sarah Barrow – Women's 10m Platform, 23rd

Alicia Blagg – Women's 3m Synchronised Springboard, 6th

Tonia Couch – Women's 10m Platform, 12th; Women's 10m Synchronised Platform, 5th

Tom Daley – Men's 10m Platform, 18th; Men's 10m Synchronised Platform, Bronze

Rebecca Gallantree – Women's 3m Springboard, 20th; Women's 3m Synchronised Springboard, 6th

Daniel Goodfellow – Men's 10m Synchronised Platform, Bronze

Jack Laugher – Men's 3m Springboard, Silver; Men's 3m Synchronised Springboard, Gold

Chris Mears – Men's 3m Synchronised Springboard, Gold

Grace Reid – Women's 3m Springboard, 8th

Lois Toulson – Women's 10m Synchronised Platform, 5th

Freddie Woodward – Men's 3m Springboard, 19th

SWIMMING

Craig Benson – Men's 200m Breaststroke, 13th

Jack Burnell – Men's 10km Open Water, Disqualified

Jazz Carlin – Women's 400m Freestyle, Silver; Women's 800m Freestyle, Silver

Georgia Coates – Women's 200m Freestyle, 27th; Women's 4x100m Medley Relay, 7th

Georgia Davies – Women's 100m Backstroke, 10th; Women's 4x100m Medley Relay, 7th

Eleanor Faulkner – Women's 200m Freestyle, 32nd

James Guy – Men's 200m Freestyle, 4th; Men's 400m Freestyle, 6th; Men's 100m Butterfly, 14th; Men's 4x200m Freestyle Relay, Silver; Men's 4x100m Medley Relay, Silver

Fran Halsall – Women's 50m Freestyle, 4th; Women's 4x100m Medley Relay, 7th

Camilla Hattersley – Women's 800m Freestyle, 15th

Cameron Kurle – Men's 200m Freestyle, 35th

Max Litchfield – Men's 400m Individual Medley, 4th

Ieuan Lloyd – Men's 200m Individual Medley, 10th

Hannah Miley – Women's 200m Individual Medley, 12th, Women's 400m Individual Medley, 4th

Stephen Milne – Men's 400m Freestyle, 13th; Men's 1500m Freestyle, 10th, Men's 4x200m Freestyle Relay, Silver

Ross Murdoch – Men's 100m Breaststroke, 11th

Siobhan-Marie O'Connor – Women's 200m Individual Medley, Silver; Women's 4x100m Medley Relay, 7th

Keri-anne Payne – Women's 10km Open Water, 7th

Adam Peaty – Men's 100m Breaststroke, Gold; Men's 4x100m Medley Relay, Silver

Ben Proud – Men's 100m Freestyle, 29th

Molly Renshaw – Women's 100m Breaststroke, 23rd; Women's 200m Breaststroke, 6th

Robbie Renwick – Men's 4x200m Freestyle Relay, Silver

Duncan Scott – Men's 100m Freestyle, 5th; Men's 4x200m Freestyle Relay, Silver; Men's 4x100m Medley Relay, Silver

Tim Shuttleworth – Men's 1500m Freestyle, 27th

Chloe Tutton – Women's 100m Breaststroke, 14th; Women's 200m Breaststroke, 4th; Women's 4x100m Medley Relay, 7th

Chris Walker-Hebborn – Men's 100m Backstroke, 11th; Men's 4x100m Medley Relay, Silver

Dan Wallace – Men's 200m Individual Medley, 8th; Men's 4x200m Freestyle Relay, Silver

Andrew Willis – Men's 200m Breaststroke, 4th

Aimee Willmott – Women's 200m Butterfly, 19th; Women's 400m Individual Medley, 7th

SYNCHRONISED SWIMMING

Katie Clark – Duet, 17th

Olivia Federici – Duet, 17th

ARCHERY

Naomi Folkard – Women's Individual, Quarter-finals

Patrick Huston – Men's Individual, Round of 32

ATHLETICS

Margaret Adeoye – Women's 4x400m Relay, Bronze

Harry Aikines-Aryeetey – Men's 4x100m Relay, 5th

Jessica Andrews – Women's 10,000m, 16th

Dina Asher-Smith – Women's 200m, 5th; Women's 4x100m Relay, Bronze

Chris Baker – Men's High Jump, Qualifying round

Chris Bennett – Men's Hammer, Qualifying round

Tom Bosworth – Men's 20km Race Walk, 6th

Holly Bradshaw – Women's Pole Vault, 5th

Seren Bundy-Davies – Women's 400m, Round 1; Women's 4x400m Relay, Bronze

Andrew Butchart – Men's 5000m, 6th

Lawrence Clarke – Men's 110m Hurdles, Semi-finals

Luke Cutts – Men's Pole Vault, Qualifying round

James Dasaolu – Men's 100m, Semi-finals

Emily Diamond – Women's 400m, Semi-finals; Women's 4x400m Relay, Bronze

Alyson Dixon – Women's Marathon, 28th

Eilidh Doyle – Women's 400m hurdles, 8th; Women's 4x400m Relay, Bronze

Mark Dry – Men's Hammer, Qualifying round

James Ellington – Men's 100m, Round 1; Men's 4x100m Relay, 5th

Jessica Ennis-Hill – Women's Heptathlon, Silver

Mo Farah – Men's 5000m, Gold; Men's 10,000m, Gold

Tom Farrell – Men's 5000m, Round 1

Adam Gemili – Men's 200m, 4th; Men's 4x100m Relay, 5th

Elliot Giles – Men's 800m, Round 1

Robbie Grabarz – Men's High Jump, 4th

Jack Green – Men's 400m Hurdles, Semi-finals

Charlie Grice – Men's 1500m, 12th

Callum Hawkins – Men's Marathon, 9th

Derek Hawkins – Men's Marathon, 114th

Desiree Henry – Women's 100m, Semi-finals; Women's 4x100m Relay, Bronze

Sophie Hitchon – Women's Hammer, Bronze

Matthew Hudson-Smith – Men's 400m, 8th; Men's 4x400m Relay, DQ

Katarina Johnson-Thompson – Women's Heptathlon, 6th

Richard Kilty – Men's 4x100m Relay, 5th

Dominic King – Men's 50km Race Walk, Disqualified

Morgan Lake – Women's High Jump, 10th

Jade Lally – Women's Discus, Qualifying round

Nigel Levine – Men's 4x400m Relay, DQ

Kelly Massey – Women's 4x400m Relay, Bronze

Eilish McColgan – Women's 5000m, 13th

Nick Miller – Men's Hammer, Qualifying round

Ross Millington – Men's 10,000m, 31st

Nethaneel Mitchell-Blake – Men's 200m, Semi-final

Laura Muir – Women's 1500m, 7th

Rob Mullett – Men's 3000m Steeplechase, Round 1

Daryll Neita – Women's 100m, Round 1; Women's 4x100m Relay, Bronze

Cindy Ofili – Women's 100m hurdles, 4th

Chris O'Hare – Men's 1500m, Semi-finals

Christine Ohuruogu – Women's 400m, Semi-finals; Women's 4x400m Relay, Bronze

Anyika Onuora – Women's 4x400m Relay, Bronze

Shelayna Oskan-Clarke – Women's 800m, Semi-finals

Jo Pavey – Women's 10,000m, 15th

Asha Philip – Women's 100m, Semi-finals; Women's 4x100m Relay, Bronze

Tiffany Porter – Women's 100m hurdles, 7th

Beth Potter – Women's 10,000m, 34th

Andy Pozzi – Men's 110m Hurdles, Semi-finals

Shara Proctor – Women's Long Jump, Qualifying round

Michael Rimmer – Men's 800m, Semi-finals

Sebastian Rodger – Men's 400m Hurdles, Round 1

Martyn Rooney – Men's 400m, Round 1; Men's 4x400m Relay, DQ

Greg Rutherford – Men's Long Jump, Bronze

Sonia Samuels – Women's Marathon, 30th

Jazmin Sawyers – Women's Long Jump, 8th

Lynsey Sharp – Women's 800m, 6th

Daniel Talbot – Men's 200m, Semi-final

Tsegai Tewelde – Men's Marathon, DNF

Stephanie Twell – Women's 5000m, Round 1

Lorraine Ugen – Women's Long Jump, 11th

Chijindu Ujah – Men's 100m, Semi-finals; Men's 4x100m Relay, 5th

Andy Vernon – Men's 10,000m, 25th

Lennie Waite – Women's 3000m Steeplechase, Round 1

Laura Weightman – Women's 1500m, 11th

Laura Whittle – Women's 5000m, Round 1

Delano Williams – Men's 4x400m Relay, DQ

Jodie Williams – Women's 200m, Semi-finals

BADMINTON

Chris Adcock – Mixed Doubles, Group stage

Gabby Adcock – Mixed Doubles, Group stage

Marcus Ellis – Men's Doubles, Bronze

Kirsty Gilmour – Women's Singles, Group stage

Chris Langridge – Men's Doubles, Bronze

Heather Olver – Women's Doubles, Group stage

Rajiv Ouseph – Men's Singles, Quarter-finals

Lauren Smith – Women's Doubles, Group stage

BOXING

Nicola Adams – Women's Flyweight, Gold

Muhammad Ali – Men's Flyweight, Round of 16

Qais Ashfaq – Men's Bantamweight, Round of 32

Joshua Buatsi – Men's Light-Heavyweight, Bronze

Joe Cordina – Men's Lightweight, Round of 16

Antony Fowler – Men's Middleweight, Round of 32

Joe Joyce – Men's Super-Heavyweight, Silver

Josh Kelly – Men's Welterweight, Round of 16

Savannah Marshall – Women's Middleweight, Quarter-finals

Pat McCormack – Men's Light-Welterweight, Round of 16

Lawrence Okolie – Men's Heavyweight, Round of 16

Galal Yafai – Men's Light-Flyweight, Round of 16

CANOEING

CANOE SLALOM

Joe Clarke – Men's K1, Gold

David Florence – Men's C1, 10th; Men's C2, Silver

Richard Hounslow – Men's C2, Silver

Fiona Pennie – Women's K1, 6th

CANOE SPRINT

Lani Belcher – K2 500m, 7th B final

Rachel Cawthorn – K1 500m, 7th B final; K4 500m, 7th

Louisa Gurski – K4 500m, 7th

Angela Hannah – K2 500m, 7th B final

Liam Heath – K1 200m, Gold; K2 200m, Silver

Jon Schofield – K2 200m, Silver

Rebeka Simon – K4 500m, 7th

Jess Walker – K1 200m, 7th B final; K4 500m, 7th

CYCLING

TRACK CYCLING

Katie Archibald – Women's Team Pursuit, Gold

Elinor Barker – Women's Team Pursuit, Gold

Steven Burke – Men's Team Pursuit, Gold

Mark Cavendish – Men's Omnium, Silver; Men's Team Pursuit, Gold

Ed Clancy – Men's Team Pursuit, Gold

Owain Doull – Men's Team Pursuit, Gold

Philip Hindes – Men's Team Sprint, Gold

Rebecca James – Women's Sprint, Silver; Women's Keirin, Silver

Jason Kenny – Men's Team Sprint, Gold; Men's Individual Sprint, Gold; Men's Keirin, Gold

Katy Marchant – Women's Sprint, Bronze

Joanna Rowsell Shand – Women's Team Pursuit, Gold

Callum Skinner – Men's Team Sprint, Gold; Men's Sprint, Silver; Men's Keirin, Round 1

Laura Trott – Women's Team Pursuit, Gold; Women's Omnium, Gold

Bradley Wiggins – Men's Team Pursuit, Gold

ROAD CYCLING

Lizzie Armitstead – Women's Road Race, 5th

Steve Cummings – Men's Road Race, DNF

Chris Froome – Men's Road Race, 12th; Men's Time Trial, Bronze

Nikki Harris – Women's Road Race, 52nd

Emma Pooley – Women's Road Race, 53rd; Women's Time Trial, 14th

Ian Stannard – Men's Road Race, DNF

Geraint Thomas – Men's Road Race, 11th; Men's Time Trial, 9th

Adam Yates – Men's Road Race, 15th

BMX

Kyle Evans – Men's Individual, Quarter-finals

Liam Phillips – Men's Individual, Quarter-finals

MOUNTAIN BIKE

Grant Ferguson – Men's Cross-Country, 17th

EQUESTRIAN

EVENTING

William Fox-Pitt – Individual, 12th; Team 5th

Pippa Funnell – Individual, 26th; Team 5th

Kitty King – Individual, 30th; Team 5th

Gemma Tattersall – Individual, 41st; Team 5th

DRESSAGE

Fiona Bigwood – Individual, 17th; Team, Silver

Charlotte Dujardin – Individual, Gold; Team, Silver

Carl Hester – Individual, 7th; Team, Silver

Spencer Wilton – Team, Silver

JUMPING

Ben Maher – Individual, 25th; Team, 12th

Nick Skelton – Individual, Gold; Team, 12th

John Whitaker – Individual, 57th; Team, 12th

Michael Whitaker – Individual, 45th; Team, 12th

FENCING

James Davis – Men's Individual Foil, Round of 16; Men's Team Foil, 6th

Laurence Halsted – Men's Individual Foil, Round of 32; Men's Team Foil, 6th

Richard Kruse – Men's Individual Foil, 4th; Men's Team Foil, 6th

Marcus Mepstead – Men's Team Foil, 6th

GOLF

Charley Hull – Women's Individual, T7th

Catriona Matthew – Women's Individual, 29th

Justin Rose – Men's Individual, Gold

Danny Willett – Men's Individual, T37th

GYMNASTICS

ARTISTIC

Brinn Bevan – Men's Team All-Around, 4th; Men's Individual All-Around, 17th; Men's Pommel Horse, 19th; Men's Parallel Bars, 27th; Men's Rings, 31st; Men's Horizontal Bar, 31st; Men's Floor Exercise, 36th

Becky Downie – Women's Team All-Around, 5th; Women's Uneven Bars, 10th; Women's Beam, 52nd

Ellie Downie – Women's Team All-Around, 5th; Women's Vault, 11th; Women's Beam, 11th; Women's Individual All-Around, 13th; Women's Uneven Bars, 26th; Women's Floor Exercise, 72nd

Claudia Fragapane – Women's Team All-Around, 5th; Women's Floor Exercise, 11th; Women's Individual All-Around, 30th; Women's Beam, 48th; Women's Uneven Bars, 69th

Ruby Harrold – Women's Team All-Around, 5th; Women's Uneven Bars, 19th; Women's Floor Exercise, 35th

Louis Smith – Men's Pommel Horse, Silver; Men's Team All-Around, 4th

Kristian Thomas – Men's Team All-Around, 4th; Men's Floor Exercise, 7th; Men's Horizontal Bar, 13th; Men's Rings, 38th

Amy Tinkler – Women's Floor Exercise, Bronze; Women's Team All-Around, 5th; Women's Beam, 12th

Max Whitlock – Men's Floor Exercise, Gold; Men's Pommel Horse, Gold; Men's Individual All-Around, Bronze; Men's Team All-Around, 4th; Men's Rings, 22nd; Men's Parallel Bars, 23rd; Men's Horizontal Bar, 58th

Nile Wilson – Men's Horizontal Bar, Bronze; Men's Team All-Around, 4th; Men's Individual All-Around, 8th; Men's Floor Exercise, 13th; Men's Rings, 14th; Men's Parallel Bars, 34th; Men's Pommel Horse, 38th

TRAMPOLINE

Nathan Bailey – Men's Individual, 9th

Kat Driscoll – Women's Individual, 6th

Bryony Page – Women's Individual, Silver

HOCKEY

Women's Tournament, Gold
Squad: **Giselle Ansley, Sophie Bray, Crista Cullen, Alex Danson, Maddie Hinch, Hannah Macleod, Shona McCallin, Lily Owsley, Sam Quek, Helen Richardson-Walsh, Kate Richardson-Walsh, Susannah Townsend, Georgie Twigg, Laura Unsworth, Hollie Webb, Nicola White.**

Men's Tournament, Group Stage
Squad: **David Ames, Alastair Brogdon, Nicolas Catlin, David Condon, Adam Dixon, Daniel Fox, Mark Gleghorne, Michael Hoare, Ashley Jackson, Iain Lewers, Simon Mantell, Harry Martin, Barry Middleton, George Pinner, Ian Sloan, Samuel Ward, Henry Weir.**

JUDO

Sally Conway – Women's -70kg, Bronze

Benjamin Fletcher – Men's -100g, Round of 32

Ashley McKenzie – Men's -60kg, Round of 16

Colin Oates – Men's -66kg, Round of 32

Natalie Powell – Women's -78kg, Quarter-finals

Alice Schlesinger – Women's -63kg, Round of 16

Nekoda Smythe-Davis – Women's -57kg, Round of 16

MODERN PENTATHLON

Joe Choong – Men's Individual, 10th

James Cooke – Men's Individual, 14th

Kate French – Women's Individual, 6th

Samantha Murray – Women's Individual, 9th

ROWING

Mark Aldred – Men's Lightweight Coxless Four, Semi-finals

Chris Bartley – Men's Lightweight Coxless Four, Semi-finals

Jack Beaumont – Men's Quadruple Sculls, 5th

Karen Bennett – Women's Coxed Eight, Silver

Paul Bennett – Men's Coxed Eight, Gold

Alan Campbell – Men's Single Sculls, Semi-finals

Olivia Carnegie-Brown – Women's Coxed Eight, Silver

Peter Chambers – Men's Lightweight Coxless Four, Semi-finals

Richard Chambers – Men's Lightweight Double Sculls, Semi-finals

Jono Clegg – Men's Lightweight Coxless Four, Semi-finals

John Collins – Men's Double Sculls, 5th

Katherine Copeland – Women's Lightweight Double Sculls, Repechage

Zoe de Toledo – Women's Coxed Eight, Silver

Scott Durant – Men's Coxed Eight, Gold

Jessica Eddie – Women's Coxed Eight, Silver

Will Fletcher – Men's Lightweight Double Sculls, Semi-finals

Helen Glover – Women's Coxless Pair, Gold

Matt Gotrel – Men's Coxed Eight, Gold

Katherine Grainger – Women's Double Sculls, Silver

Alex Gregory – Men's Coxless Four, Gold

Katie Greves – Women's Coxed Eight, Silver

Angus Groom – Men's Quadruple Sculls, 5th

Phelan Hill – Men's Coxed Eight, Gold

Frances Houghton – Women's Coxed Eight, Silver

Stewart Innes – Men's Coxless Pair, 4th

Peter Lambert – Men's Quadruple Sculls, 5th

Matt Langridge – Men's Coxed Eight, Gold

Zoe Lee – Women's Coxed Eight, Silver

Constantine Louloudis – Men's Coxless Four, Gold

George Nash – Men's Coxless Four, Gold

Tom Ransley – Men's Coxed Eight, Gold

Pete Reed – Men's Coxed Eight, Gold

William Satch – Men's Coxed Eight, Gold

Mohamed Sbihi – Men's Coxless Four, Gold

Alan Sinclair – Men's Coxless Pair, 4th

Heather Stanning – Women's Coxless Pair, Gold

Polly Swann – Women's Coxed Eight, Silver

Charlotte Taylor – Women's Lightweight Double Sculls, Repechage

Victoria Thornley – Women's Double Sculls, Silver

Sam Townsend – Men's Quadruple Sculls, 5th

Andrew Triggs Hodge – Men's Coxed Eight, Gold

Jonathan Walton – Men's Double Sculls, 5th

Melanie Wilson – Women's Coxed Eight, Silver

RUGBY SEVENS

Men's Tournament, Silver
Squad: **Mark Bennett, Dan Bibby, Phil Burgess, Sam Cross, James Davies, Ollie Lindsay Hague, Ruaridh McConnochie, Tom Mitchell, Dan Norton, James Rodwell, Mark Robertson, Marcus Watson.**

Women's Tournament, 4th
Squad: **Claire Allan, Abbie Brown, Heather Fisher, Natasha Hunt, Jasmine Joyce, Katy McLean, Alice Richardson, Emily Scarratt, Emily Scott, Danielle Waterman, Joanne Watmore, Amy Wilson-Hardy.**

SAILING

Sophie Ainsworth – Women's 49er FX, 8th

Saskia Clark – Women's 470, Gold

Nick Dempsey – Men's RS:X, Silver

Charlotte Dobson – Women's 49er FX, 8th

Dylan Fletcher – Men's 49er, 6th

Nicola Groves – Nacra 17, 9th

Chris Grube – Men's 470, 5th

Hannah Mills – Women's 470, Gold

Luke Patience – Men's 470, 5th

Ben Saxton – Nacra 17, 9th

Giles Scott – Men's Finn, Gold

Bryony Shaw – Women's RS:X, 9th

Alain Sign – Men's 49er, 6th

Nick Thompson – Men's Laser, 6th

Alison Young – Women's Laser Radial, 8th

SHOOTING

Elena Allen – Women's Skeet, 14th

Amber Hill – Women's Skeet, 6th

Tim Kneale – Men's Double Trap, 4th

Ed Ling – Men's Trap, Bronze

Jen McIntosh – Women's 10m Air Rifle, 15th; Women's 50m Rifle 3 Positions, 18th

Steven Scott – Men's Double Trap, Bronze

TABLE TENNIS

Paul Drinkhall – Men's Singles, Round 4; Men's Team, Quarter-finals

Liam Pitchford – Men's Singles, Round 3; Men's Team, Quarter-finals

Sam Walker – Men's Team, Quarter-finals

TAEKWONDO

Mahama Cho – Men's +80kg, 4th

Jade Jones – Women's -57kg, Gold

Lutalo Muhammad – Men's -80kg, Silver

Bianca Walkden – Women's +67kg, Bronze

TENNIS

Kyle Edmund – Men's Singles, Round 2

Colin Fleming – Men's Doubles, Round 1

Dom Inglot – Men's Doubles, Round 1

Johanna Konta – Women's Singles, Quarter-finals; Women's Doubles, Round 2; Mixed Doubles, Round 1

Andy Murray – Men's Singles, Gold; Mixed Doubles, Quarter-finals; Men's Doubles, Round 1

Jamie Murray – Men's Doubles, Round 1; Mixed Doubles, Round 1

Heather Watson – Women's Singles, Round 2; Women's Doubles, Round 2; Mixed Doubles, Quarter-finals

TRIATHLON

Gordon Benson – Men's Individual, DNF

Alistair Brownlee – Men's Individual, Gold

Jonny Brownlee – Men's Individual, Silver

Vicky Holland – Women's Individual, Bronze

Helen Jenkins – Women's Individual, 19th

Non Stanford – Women's Individual, 4th

WEIGHTLIFTING

Rebekah Tiler – Women's 69kg, 10th

Sonny Webster – Men's 94kg, 14th

Right: Team GB athletes pose next to the British Airways Boeing 747 with its nose painted gold and renamed "victoRIOus".

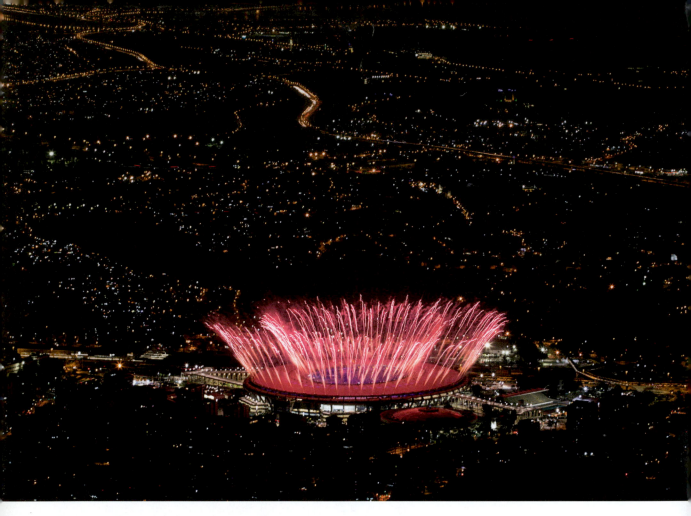

Acknowledgements

PRESS ASSOCIATION SPORT

Editors: Andrew McDermott, Stuart Walker.

Contributors: Guy Aspin, Liam Blackburn, Dave Clark, Eleanor Crooks, Ed Elliot, Wayne Gardiner, Phil Medlicott, Ian Parker, Euan Parsons, Chris Phillips, Glen Robertson, Matt Somerford, Mark Staniforth, Karen Sykes, Mark Walker, Declan Warrington, Tom White, Jim van Wijk.

Production: Mark Tattersall, Steve White, Chris Wiltshire.

Picture research: Dominic Picksley.

PICTURES

Press Association Images/Associated Press.

The scene at the Maracana Stadium during the Closing Ceremony as fireworks go off to match those produced by Team GB throughout an historic Olympic Games.